Buckle Down.

to the
Common Core
State Standards
English Language Arts
Grade 8

This book belongs to: _____

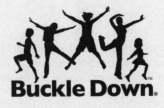

Buckle Down.

Helping your schoolhouse meet the standards of the statehouse™

Acknowledgment

The Common Core Standards were developed by the National Governors Association Center for Best Practices (NGA Center) and the Council of Chief State School Officers (CCSSO) in collaboration with teachers, school administrators, and experts.

Every effort has been made by the publisher to locate each owner of the copyrighted material reprinted in this publication and to secure the necessary permissions. If there are any questions regarding the use of these materials, the publisher will take appropriate corrective measures to acknowledge ownership in future publications.

ISBN 978-0-7836-8054-5

1CCUS08RD01   1 2 3 4 5 6 7 8 9 10

Cover Image: Winding road through the forest in the Appalachian Mountains. © Alexey Stiop/Dreamstime.com

Triumph Learning® 136 Madison Avenue, 7th Floor, New York, NY 10016

© 2011 Triumph Learning, LLC
Buckle Down is an imprint of Triumph Learning®

Frequently Asked Questions about the Common Core State Standards

What are the Common Core Standards?

The Common Core Standards for English Language Arts, grades K–12, are a set of shared goals and expectations for what knowledge and skills will help students succeed. They allow students to understand what is expected of them and to become progressively more proficient in understanding and using English Language Arts. At the same time, teachers will be better equipped to know exactly what they need to help students learn and establish individualized benchmarks for them.

Will the Common Core Standards tell teachers how and what to teach?

No. The best understanding of what works in the classroom comes from the teachers who are in them. That's why these standards will establish *what* students need to learn, but they will not dictate *how* teachers should teach. Instead, schools and teachers will decide how best to help students reach the standards.

What will the Common Core Standards mean for students?

The standards will provide more clarity about and consistency in what is expected of student learning across the country. Common standards will not prevent different levels of achievement among students, but they will ensure more consistent exposure to materials and learning experiences through curriculum, instruction, and teacher preparation among other supports for student learning. These standards will help prepare students with the knowledge and skills they need to succeed in college and careers.

Do the Common Core Standards focus on skills and content knowledge?

Yes. The Common Core Standards recognize that both content and skills are important. The Common Core Standards contain rigorous content and application of knowledge through high-order thinking skills. The English Language Arts standards require certain critical content for all students, including: classic myths and stories from around the world, America's founding documents, foundational American literature, and Shakespeare. The remaining crucial decisions about what content should be taught are left to state and local determination. In addition to content coverage, the Common Core Standards require that students systematically acquire knowledge in literature and other disciplines through reading, writing, speaking, and listening.

The Common Core Standards also require that students develop a depth of understanding and ability to apply English Language Arts to novel situations, as college students and employees regularly do.

Will common assessments be developed? When will they be ready?

It will be up to the states: some states plan to come together voluntarily to develop a common assessment system. A state-led consortium on assessment would be grounded in the following principles: allow for comparison across students, schools, districts, states, and nations; create economies of scale; provide information and support more effective teaching and learning; and prepare students for college and careers.

A common assessment could be in place in some states by the 2014–2015 school year.

TABLE OF CONTENTS

To the Teacher:

Common Core Standards are listed for each lesson in the table of contents and for each page in the shaded gray bars that run across the tops of the pages in the workbook (see the example at right).

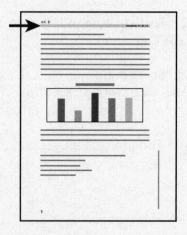

Reading

Some people think reading is an all-or-nothing deal: either you're good at it or you're not. But that's not true. There are things you can do to improve your skills as a reader, even if you're a good reader already.

Think of it this way: Have you ever watched a building rise? From an empty lot to a finished house, it all starts with a strong foundation. Without a strong foundation, floors will sink, walls will crumble, and the building cannot stand.

Reading is like this, too. You need a foundation for successful reading. This foundation starts with vocabulary and basic reading skills, like finding the main idea of a story or understanding an author's reason for writing. In this unit, you will focus on these skills and build your own strong foundation for reading.

In This Unit

Vocabulary

Main Idea and Details

Reading Strategies

Nonfiction

Stories and Drama

Poetry

Literacy in History/ Social Studies, Science, and Technical Subjects

Lesson 1: Vocabulary

The English language is made up of thousands of words. As a reader, you may wonder how anyone can be expected to keep track of so many words. Do you have to spend your nights reading the dictionary in order to understand all the things you read? The simple answer is: no.

In this lesson, we'll review some of the ways you can figure out the meanings of words as you read. This involves understanding where words come from and how they are built, and analyzing how words are used in context. Your new vocabulary skills will help you navigate even the trickiest text.

Word Origins and Structures

In English class, one of the things you practice is mastering the conventions of the English language—spelling, grammar, usage, and punctuation. While it's important to know these rules, it's also good to keep in mind that some of them have not always existed. Knowing a word's origin and structure can help us understand its meaning. **Origin** is the beginning of something. **Structure** is the way words are put together.

Many words are made up of **roots**, or base words with simple meanings. **Affixes** are word parts that are added to roots to change their meanings. There are two kinds of affixes. A **prefix** is a word part that is added to the beginning of a root word to form a new word. Recognizing a prefix can help you figure out the meaning of an unknown word. A **suffix** is added to the end of a root word. Sometimes the spelling of the root word will change when a suffix is added. Learning some common word parts will give you insight into the meanings they create when they are combined.

Take, for example, the word *antidisestablishmentarianism*. (Yes, it's a real word!) At the heart of the word is the root *establish*. You probably know that this word means "to make" or "to set up." Two prefixes have been added to the beginning of the root, and three suffixes have been added to the end:

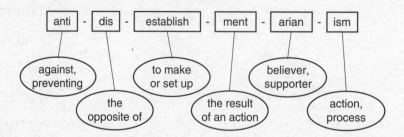

All these parts add up to create a word that means "a movement against the people who oppose the established order."

CCSs: L.8.4a, L.8.4b

In this lesson, you will learn to find elements of the history of English in many familiar words. You will also practice breaking unfamiliar words into parts to figure out their meanings. With a little knowledge about word parts—and a little practice—you can take apart thousands of affixed words and work out their meanings.

A Living Language

Though you might expect it to be dry or dull, the history of English is a stirring tale of the people who have spoken it. The time line that follows gives a sense of the sweeping story of English.

History of English

ca. 700 BCE
Celts settle in England. **Celtic** is spoken.

55 BCE
Julius Caesar invades England. His invasion is a failure.

43 CE
Roman emperor Claudius conquers England. **Latin** is spoken by military and ruling class for 400 years.

410
Roman troops withdraw. Latin influence fades fast.

450–550
Germanic invasion: Angles, Saxons, and Jutes arrive, bringing a language that becomes known as English (**Old English**). They write in runes, alphabetic characters that also have meaning as words. Celts retreat to Wales and Ireland.

ca. 600
Christian missionaries arrive in England, bringing the **Roman alphabet**.

ca. 800
Viking invasions begin, bringing Norse words into the language.

1066
Norman invasion: William the Conqueror arrives from northern France. Old French, a language close to Latin, is spoken in the court. **Middle English**, containing many French words, emerges among the people.

1476
William Caxton brings the printing press (invented around 1440) to England. Birth of **Modern English** and the Renaissance Period.

1476–1603
English Renaissance: Revival of **ancient Greek** learning brings Greek words, such as *democracy*, into the language.

1521
Spaniard Cortéz conquers Aztecs in Mexico. **Spanish** influence later advances into Texas and California.

1607
First permanent English settlement in America at Jamestown, Virginia. English encounter various native tribes and adapt **Native American** place-names.

1619
First African slaves arrive in America, bringing a mixture of African tongues that blend with English to develop into **Gullah**.

1828
Noah Webster publishes *American Dictionary of the English Language*, defining a distinct American vocabulary. Spelling becomes more standardized.

1800s–1900s
Immigrants from Ireland, Germany, Scandinavia, eastern Europe, Italy, China, Puerto Rico, Cuba, Vietnam, and Mexico add words to American English.

1920s
"Jazz Age" in New York and Chicago popularizes **African-American dialect**.

1970s–2000s
Advances in technology introduce new words into the language. Computers and spell-check programs further standardize English.

TIP 1: English has Germanic origins.

The first language that could be called English arose around 1,500 years ago. The languages of many groups, including Angles, Saxons, Jutes, and Celts, blended together to form English. Many of the words we use today contain prefixes, suffixes, or roots from these languages.

Anglo-Saxon Prefixes

Prefix	Meaning	Examples
be-	make	befriend, bewitch
fore-	before, front	forearm, forego
mis-	badly, wrongly	misconception, misdirect
out-	beyond, outside, more than	outmaneuver, outlandish
un-	not, opposite of	unconstitutional, unavailable
up-	rising, above, high	upswing, upriver, uproar
with-	back, away, against	withdraw, withhold

Anglo-Saxon Roots

Root	Meaning	Examples
bind	tie, fasten	binder
drif	carry along	drifter, adrift
fod/fed	food	feed, fodder, foster
kne	joint of the leg	knee, kneel, knicker
lack	to be without	lackadaisical
step	to stamp, to deprive	stepladder, stepmother
ster	guide, direct	steer
tru	faithful	truth, betrothed

CCSs: L.8.4a, L.8.4b

Anglo-Saxon Suffixes

Suffix	Meaning	Examples
-er	comparison, one who does something	stealthier, provider
-ful	full of, characterized by	boastful, woeful
-ish	in the manner of, relating to	brutish, impoverish
-ly	in the manner of	sheepishly, frantically
-ness	condition or state of being	greatness, laziness
-ship	condition, profession, skill	courtship, professorship

Use the previous charts to answer Numbers 1 and 2.

1. What does *foretold* mean?

    A. not told

    B. told before

    C. wrongly told

    D. faithfully told

2. Would you want to be friends with someone who is *mistrustful*? Why or why not?

    _____

    _____

    _____

    _____

TIP 2: Latin and Greek add important prefixes, suffixes, and roots.

Many of the prefixes, suffixes, and root words we use come from Latin or Greek. By keeping in mind what common Latin or Greek affixes and roots mean, you may be able to discover the meaning of an unfamiliar word.

Latin and Greek Affixes

Prefix	Source
a- (without, not)	Greek
ad-, as- (to, toward)	Latin
anti- (against, opposite)	Greek
auto- (self)	Greek
bi- (two)	Latin
cata- (down)	Greek
com- (with, together)	Latin
contra- (against, opposite)	Latin
de- (reverse, remove)	Latin
di- (two, through)	Greek
dis- (undo, not)	Latin
im-, in- (into, not)	Latin
mal- (bad)	Latin
mid- (middle)	Latin
mono- (one)	Greek
non- (not)	Latin
ob- (in the way, against)	Latin
peri- (around, about)	Greek
post- (after)	Latin
pre- (before)	Latin
pro- (forward, for)	Greek
re- (again, back)	Latin

Suffix	Source
-able, -ible (able to)	Latin
-ance (state, action)	Latin
-ant (agent, receiver)	Latin
-ary (related to)	Latin
-ation, -ion, -tion (state, process, result)	Latin
-cracy (rule of)	Greek
-graphy (writing of)	Greek
-ic (characteristic, relating to)	Latin
-ile (of, relating to)	Latin
-ity (state, quality)	Latin
-ive (quality of)	Latin
-logy, -ology (study of)	Greek
-ment (result, action)	Greek
-phobia (fear of)	Greek

CCSs: L.8.4a, L.8.4b

Latin and Greek Roots

Root	Source	Root	Source	Root	Source
acid, aci (sour)	Latin	helio (sun)	Greek	rect (straight)	Latin
andro (man)	Greek	homo (same)	Greek	sect (cut)	Latin
anthropo (human)	Greek	hydra, hydro (water)	Latin	sede (to sit)	Latin
audi (hear)	Latin	liber (free, book)	Latin	soph (wisdom)	Greek
biblio (book)	Greek	lum (light)	Latin	spect (watch, see)	Latin
bio (life)	Greek	mega (large)	Greek	stas (stand)	Greek
cede (go, yield)	Latin	meter (measure)	Greek	theo (god)	Greek
circum (around)	Latin	morph (shape)	Greek	therm (heat)	Greek
dict (speak)	Latin	omni (all)	Latin	trac(t) (draw)	Latin
duct (lead)	Latin	pater (father)	Latin	vert (turn)	Latin
fac (do, make)	Latin	patho (suffering)	Greek	vis (sight)	Latin
fer (to carry)	Latin	philo (love of)	Greek	vit (life)	Latin
gen (race, stock)	Greek	polis (city)	Greek	voca (call)	Latin
geo (rock)	Greek	pseudo (false)	Greek	vol (to fly)	Latin
gyn (woman)	Greek	psycho (mind)	Greek	volv (to roll)	Latin

And don't forget the Latin numbers:

Latin Numbers

1	2	3	4	5	6	7	8	9	10	11	12
uni-	di-	tri-	quad-	quint-	sex-	sept-	oct-	nona-	deca-	cent-	mill-

3. Choose two Greek roots and two Latin roots, and write an English word based upon each.

_____

_____

_____

_____

4. Which word means "scared of water"?

   A. hydrology

   B. hydrophobia

   C. heliographic

   D. heliolatry

5. What is the meaning of *audible*?

_____

A Global Language

Since the early seventeenth century, colonization and globalization have spread English around the world. As the language has been transplanted to new continents, it has absorbed new words and grown in different ways in each place. So, even though people in many countries speak English, some of the words they use might be unfamiliar to Americans or used in unfamiliar ways. For example, an American might stand in a *line* to buy a ticket to a concert; people in Great Britain stand in a *queue*. What you call *soccer* many people around the world call *football*. Americans purchase *gas* for their cars, New Zealanders buy *benzine,* and Australians buy *petrol.* Your family might have a *backyard barbecue*; a South African would call it a *braai.*

CCSs: L.8.4c, L.8.5b

Words in Context

Now that you know where words come from and how they are formed, you can start paying attention to how words are used in sentences.

Imagine that your dad sees you trying on your new Philadelphia Eagles jersey. He makes approving sounds and smiles to show that he thinks you look good. You probably expect him to say something like, "Hey, nice shirt!" Instead, he grins and says, "Dude, that shirt is ace. You look rad!" Huh? Did he just compliment you?

Actually, your dad said, in a 1980s sort of way, that your new shirt looks great. All you had to do to understand his message was pay attention to the clues he gave you: his smile, the approving sound he made, and the admiring tone of his voice.

It's All about Context

Figuring out the meanings of difficult words in a reading passage is a lot like learning unfamiliar slang. You can learn the meaning of the latest slang (or even your grandma's out-of-date lingo) by paying attention in a conversation. In the same way, you can learn the meaning of a written word by paying attention to its context. In reading, **context** means the surrounding words and sentences.

To see how this works, read the following sentence, and then answer Number 6.

> Never one to give up, Margo worked <u>tenaciously</u> to make the Olympic snowboarding team, and her tireless efforts finally paid off.

6. What is the meaning of the word *tenaciously* as it is used in the sentence?

    A. lazily
    B. curiously
    C. hesitantly
    D. tirelessly

Tenaciously is about as hard a word as you are likely to see on a reading test. But even if you've never seen the word before, you can figure out what it means. The other words in the sentence give it away.

Which choice would most likely describe the way Margo works? We are told that Margo is "never one to give up" and that her efforts are "tireless." These details allow you to eliminate choices A (lazily) and C (hesitantly). Of the two choices that are left, which one would most likely lead Margo to success?

As you can see, you don't have to know the meaning of every word in the dictionary to answer a vocabulary question. However, you do need to know how to use context to figure out the meanings of unfamiliar words.

Here are a few tips to help you figure out the meanings of unknown words in a reading passage.

TIP 3: Look for other words in the passage that have meanings similar to the unknown word.

The passage often will give plenty of clues about the meaning of an unknown word. For example, read the following passage.

> Taylor Swift started writing at a very young age. In the fourth grade, she won a national poetry contest, and eventually she changed her focus to songwriting. Swift has said that she started writing songs to <u>alleviate</u> the pain of not fitting in at school. Music was a way to feel better about herself. These days, Taylor Swift is a phenomenally successful musician, and millions of young fans, many of whom perhaps feel like outcasts themselves, relate to and enjoy her music.

7. Circle any words or phrases in the sentences that have a meaning similar or related to that of the underlined word.

Now read the following question. Choose the answer that is closest in meaning to the word that is underlined.

8. What is the meaning of the word *alleviate*?

   A. ease
   B. intensify
   C. worsen
   D. refresh

TIP 4: Look for causes and effects related to the unknown word.

Cause-and-effect relationships can give hints to the meaning of an unknown word. For example, use the following sentence to answer Numbers 9 and 10.

> No one ever thought that LaSalle High would beat City, so when it finally happened, the LaSalle fans were <u>euphoric</u>.

9. How do fans usually feel when their team defeats another that seems hard to beat?

_____

10. Which word is closest in meaning to *euphoric* as it is used in the example sentence?

A. satisfied

B. overjoyed

C. challenged

D. embarrassed

 TIP 5: Look for clues showing that the unknown word fits into a category.

Check to see if a word appears in a list of things or in a description of a scene. If it does, you can guess its meaning by the way it fits into the "world" that contains the other items.

Look at the following example.

> Though not as common as the barn owl, sparrow, dove, and blue jay, the <u>towhee</u> is fascinating to watch.

11. The items listed (*barn owl*, *sparrow*, *dove*, *blue jay*) all fit into what category?

_____

12. What is a *towhee*?

A. a type of tree

B. a television program

C. a kind of bird

D. a special performance

TIP 6: Look for clues that point to the opposite meaning of the unknown word.

Words such as *but*, *despite*, *although*, *surprisingly*, *not*, and *so* tend to signal a shift in the logic of a passage. Such words can hint at what a vocabulary word *doesn't* mean. This can help you make a good guess about what the word *does* mean. For example, read the following sentence and use it to answer Numbers 13 and 14.

> When Mr. Carrier first arrived in Picketsville, the townspeople thought he was a fine, upstanding, honest gentleman, but time soon showed him to be an absolute <u>rogue</u>.

13. Circle any words that describe the opposite of *rogue*.

14. What is the meaning of the word *rogue* as it is used in the passage?

    A. wise elder

    B. popular leader

    C. untrustworthy person

    D. mysterious newcomer

 TIP 7: Don't be fooled by a word with multiple-meanings.

Some vocabulary questions will test your knowledge of multiple-meaning words. These are words such as *grate*, which can mean "to scrape into small pieces," "to be hard on the nerves," or "the iron bars used to hold fire."

A multiple-choice question may list four accurate meanings for the vocabulary word. Your job will be to pick the meaning that best fits the way the word is used in the passage. For these questions, it is very important to go back to the passage and check the context before choosing your answer.

CCSs: L.8.4c, L.8.5b, L.8.5c

To see how this works, read the following sentence, and then answer Number 15.

> The reporter would not let the candidate <u>skirt</u> the issue; he asked
> her repeatedly how she planned to deal with the problem of pollution
> at Lake Murphy.

15. What is the meaning of the word *skirt* as it is used in the sentence?

   A. a woman's garment

   B. the outermost parts of a property

   C. to be on the edge of a border

   D. to avoid something

 TIP 8: Pay attention to tone.

Every word has a denotative meaning. A word's **denotative meaning** is its basic, agreed-upon definition. Many words also have connotative meanings. A word's **connotative meaning** is an extra meaning or sense it gives the reader when used in certain ways.

For example, the denotative meaning of the word *cheap* is "inexpensive," but it can also suggest that something is of low quality. This is the word's connotation. If someone says, "That's a cheap MP3 player," does that mean it doesn't cost much or that it isn't very well made? You'll need to look at the context to know for sure.

One clue that context can provide is tone. A sentence's **tone** refers to the overall emotional content of the words. A positive or negative tone can help you to understand which meaning of a word the writer intends. Read the following sentences to see how this works.

> Mom sighed as Roman brought another box to her. They had been
> shopping for hours, and Mom was tired, but when she saw the sticker on the
> box, her face lit up. "Finally!" she said. "A cheap MP3 player!"

In this context, Mom is using a positive tone. She is thrilled about the MP3 player's cheapness—its low cost.

TIP 9: Use vocabulary techniques to answer questions about figurative language and idioms.

If you say that you're so tired that your arms are limp noodles, you don't really mean that your arms are made of a flour and water substance. You are speaking figuratively rather than literally. **Figurative language** is a comparison of two things with similar qualities.

If you are having trouble understanding a figurative phrase, vocabulary strategies can sometimes help you out.

> It was hard work getting a part on the show *Reality Life*, where six born-to-clash stereotypes are placed in a posh designer home in a dream location for six months, all expenses paid. Soon the cameras would begin rolling, and the world would be able to see how young people live and get along in reality. But Nate started to wonder whether he liked the idea of <u>life under a microscope</u>, with someone, somewhere, watching his every squirming movement.

16. What does *life under a microscope* mean in this passage?

    A. a life in a house with too many other people

    B. a life with people who don't get along well

    C. a life in a place that is far away from home

    D. a life that is filmed and broadcast on television

Common Word Relationships

Here are some common types of word relationships:

antonym ("is the opposite of") *veteran : rookie*

synonym ("is the same as") *nobility : aristocracy*

characteristic ("is a characteristic of") *hope : optimist*

classification ("is a type of") *pastel : color*

degree ("is a greater/lesser degree of") *elated : happy*

cause/effect ("is the cause of") *wit : laughter*

effect/cause ("is an effect of") *devastation : hurricane*

function ("is used to") *speedometer : speed*

location ("is a place where") *museum : artifacts*

relative size ("is bigger/smaller than") *mountain : hill*

whole-to-part or **part-to-whole** ("is a part of") *trumpeter : band*

sequence ("comes before/after") *planting : harvest*

CCSs: L.8.4a, L.8.4c, L.8.4d, L.8.5a

An **idiom** is a common expression or saying. You can use vocabulary strategies to answer questions about idioms.

> Elwood was <u>down in the dumps</u> after his girlfriend broke up with him. He couldn't eat; he couldn't sleep. He just moped around all day, wondering why he had been such a jerk.

17. What does *down in the dumps* mean in this sentence?

    A. left all alone

    B. very unhappy

    C. at the bottom of a hill

    D. angry and spiteful

You will learn more about figurative language in Lesson 6.

 ## TIP 10: Build your vocabulary using a dictionary, glossary, or thesaurus.

When you aren't sure about the meaning of a word in your everyday reading, take the time to look it up in a dictionary. A **dictionary** is a very long list of words and definitions. You can't use a dictionary when you take a test, but using a dictionary is a great way to build your vocabulary as you get ready for a test. It's a habit that will help you throughout your life.

A dictionary entry can provide quite a bit of useful information. In addition to the word's correct spelling (and alternate spelling, if there is an accepted one), the entry states the word's pronunciation (including which syllable receives emphasis), its meaning or meanings, its part of speech, and often its etymology. **Etymology** is the history of a word, including where the word originated. Learning a word's etymology is interesting—it can teach you about the different cultures that contribute to the English language and how meanings change over time.

When you come across an unknown word in a nonfiction book, you can often look up the word's meaning without going to a dictionary. Many nonfiction books contain a **glossary**—a list of the difficult or unusual words in a book and definitions for those words. Glossaries are usually found at the end of books. Here is an example of a partial glossary from a book about birds of prey:

Book of Birds Glossary

mantle: upper surfaces of the wings and back

migratory: animals that move to another region when the seasons change

mottled: marked with patches of different colors

nocturnal: active during the night

pellets: small, ball-shaped objects that owls spit out, made from food parts that they cannot digest

plumes: large, showy feathers

predator: an animal that eats another animal

Another resource that you can use to figure out what a word means is a thesaurus. A **thesaurus** is a list of synonyms. A thesaurus entry may also include antonyms, as well as a brief definition. Here's what you might see if you looked up the word *prey* in a thesaurus:

Prey: noun. Definition: target. Synonyms: casualty, chase, fall guy, game, martyr, spoil, sufferer, underdog, victim. Antonyms: hunter, predator.

Even when you look up a word in a dictionary, glossary, or thesaurus, you may not always remember its exact meaning the next time you see it. But the more you read, look up words, and practice the tips in this lesson, the more your vocabulary will grow.

Lesson Practice begins on the following page.

Directions: This passage is about the man who first used the term "rock 'n' roll." Read the passage. Then answer Numbers 1 through 4.

"Moondog" Freed: Rock 'N' Roll Pioneer

by Hamilton West

Did you know that the term "rock 'n' roll" was first used by an Ohio deejay named Alan Freed? Freed had a huge influence on the music industry and on music history itself. Perhaps most important, many musicians and historians credit Freed with dismantling racial barriers during the 1950s and paving the way for equality among performers.

Freed had not yet gained celebrity status when he landed his first radio job in Pennsylvania in 1942. After gaining a year of experience, he moved to Youngstown, Ohio, to become the sportscaster on radio station WKBN. But Freed was more interested in music than in sports broadcasting, so he relocated to Akron, Ohio, in 1945 and hosted a jazz and pop show. He soon became a local celebrity.

In 1951, a Cleveland record-store owner named Leo Mintz convinced Freed to be a deejay for a rhythm-and-blues show. Freed gave himself the nickname "Moondog" and began playing music by African American musicians such as Little Richard and Chuck Berry. Though Freed was not the first person to play rock music on the radio, he is credited with coining the term "rock 'n' roll." In 1952 he organized the first-ever rock concert, "The Moondog Coronation Ball," which was attended primarily by African Americans. The concert was such a runaway success that it ended early because of overcrowding.

At a time when America was still stratified along racial lines, Freed promoted the tremendous talents of African American musicians. Many of those musicians have praised Freed for emphasizing the importance of racial harmony to American kids, even as those teens' parents clung to their old, prejudiced ways. Freed even appeared in several major films about popular African American musicians, including *Rock Around the Clock*, *Mr. Rock and Roll* (which featured Little Richard) and *Go, Johnny, Go!* (with Chuck Berry).

Following the success of these movies, Freed was booked on the European station Radio Luxembourg, where his prerecorded shows were broadcast to a wide audience. Record companies bought air time on Radio Luxembourg to promote the albums of African American musicians. These sounds were heard all across Europe— including in the town of Liverpool, England, where members of a then-unknown group called The Beatles were writing their first songs.

Most people remember Freed for working to bring down racial barriers and promote the talent of African American musicians. American music owes a lot to Alan Freed, from the success of people such as Chuck Berry to the term "rock 'n' roll" itself.

1. **The author credits Moondog Freed with "dismantling racial barriers during the 1950s." What does** *dismantling* **mean?**

   A. collapsing

   B. building

   C. holding up

   D. taking apart

2. **The word** *prerecorded* <u>**most likely**</u> **means**

   A. recorded before

   B. recorded for

   C. recorded first

   D. recorded again

3. **Read the following sentence from the passage.**

   "Though Freed was not the first person to play rock music on the radio, he is credited with coining the term 'rock 'n' roll.'"

   What is the meaning of *coining* **as it is used in this passage?**

   A. speaking

   B. claiming

   C. inventing

   D. imagining

4. In paragraph 4, the author states, "At a time when America was still stratified along racial lines, Freed promoted the tremendous talents of African American musicians." What is the <u>best</u> definition for the word *stratified* as it is used in this context? Use details from the passage to explain your answer.

_____

_____

_____

_____

_____

_____

_____

Lesson 2: Main Idea and Details

It's Monday morning. You're on your way to English class when your friend Herman catches up with you. As usual, he wants to know what the assignment was. You tell him that it was to read a short story called "My First Goose" by the famous Russian writer Isaac Babel.

You both know that your English teacher, Ms. Austen, likes to ask questions like this at the beginning of class: "Herman, what was 'My First Goose' mainly about?" Herman can be pretty annoying, but he is your friend. He may have to say something in class. You need to quickly describe the story for him in a few words.

You had read the story the night before while your family watched a rerun of *Glee*. You actually liked the story, and not just because there's a scene where a guy steps on a goose. You've been thinking it over; there's a lot to this story. You find yourself describing it to Herman in a British accent:

> "The story 'My First Goose' dramatizes the emotional conflicts of its narrator, a young intellectual assigned to a Cossack division of the Russian Army. This young man wants to be accepted by the other soldiers, who are always ready for violence. They make fun of him, however, calling him 'one of those grinds,' a book reader. The young soldier eventually wins them over by killing a goose for dinner. This violent act gains him the acceptance of his comrades, but it also fills him with great sorrow.
>
> "Babel, who lived from 1894 to 1940, was a master of the short story form. This story, barely four pages long, demonstrates his ability to suggest whole worlds—including the political atmosphere of the Russian Revolution—in a few words."

Herman stares at you for a moment, then says, "So, it's basically about an army guy who has a pet goose?"

You decide you'd better switch to a different style, one of fewer words. To help you boil down your response, let's turn this into a multiple-choice question:

1. What brief sentence would best explain to Herman the main idea of "My First Goose"?

    A. It's about a man who joins the Russian Army, then wishes he hadn't.

    B. It's about an unlucky goose that gets eaten by a group of violent Cossack soldiers.

    C. It's about a soldier who is looked down upon by his fellow soldiers for reading too much and being a brain.

    D. It's about a Russian soldier who wants to gain the acceptance of the other men in his unit.

CCSs: RL.8.2, RI.8.2, RI.8.5, RI.8.10

The **main idea** is what a passage is mostly about. In this lesson, you will practice finding the main idea of a reading passage. You'll also learn to identify the theme. The **theme** of a passage is the essential message the author is trying to get across.

 TIP 1: Preview the passage and make predictions.

You can begin to get a feel for the passage before you even start reading. By **previewing** the passage, you can get an idea about the topic, or subject, of the writing. You may be able to learn other things about the passage, as well. Preview the passage by doing the following:

- Read the title.
- Look at the illustrations.
- Read any introductory information, sidebars, and other text features.
- Skim any headings, subheadings, and words in boldface or italic type.

Once you have previewed the passage, take a guess at what the passage will be about.

2. Preview the passage from *20,000 Leagues Under the Sea* on the next page. What do you think the topic will be?

_____

3. Based on the title and introductory paragraph, what do you think will happen in the passage?

_____

_____

Previewing the passage will not only help you know what to expect but will also get your mind ready for reading. You'll be more likely to understand what you read and to remember the important ideas later.

CCSs: RL.8.10, RI.8.5

As you read the following passage, don't focus on memorizing details; simply try to understand "the big picture," or what the story is mostly about.

adapted from
20,000 Leagues Under the Sea
by Jules Verne

Just then a vast cave appeared before us, hollowed out in a picturesque pile of rock covered with all the lovely tapestry work of underwater vegetation. At first it seemed to me very dark inside this cave. The sun's rays appeared to lose their strength little by little. Their vague transparency became only a dim, blurred light.

Captain Nemo entered and we followed. My eyes soon became accustomed to the relative darkness. I could make out natural pillars supporting a whimsically shaped vaulting, and resting on a granite base, like the heavy columns of Tuscan architecture. Why was our strange guide taking us into the depths of this underwater crypt? I was soon to know.

After going down a rather steep slope, we found ourselves standing at the bottom of a sort of circular pit. There Captain Nemo stopped and pointed to something I had not noticed.

It was an oyster of amazing size, a giant clam which could have made a holy-water basin big enough to hold a lake. It was seven feet wide and therefore even bigger than the one in the Nautilus' lounge.

I went over to this phenomenal mollusk. He was fastened to a slab of granite, living all alone in the calm waters of the grotto. I calculated that this giant clam must have weighed about 650 pounds. Such an oyster must have contained 35 pounds of flesh, and it would have taken the stomach of a Gargantua to digest several dozen of these.

It was obvious Captain Nemo already knew this creature was here. It wasn't the first time he had paid it a visit. But I was wrong in thinking he had brought us here just to show us a wonder of nature. Captain Nemo had a particular reason for wanting to see how this giant clam was getting along.

The creature's two valves were partly open. The captain inserted his dagger to prevent them from closing again; then with his hand he lifted up the fringed membranes which formed the animal's cloak.

There, among the leaflike folds, I saw a loose pearl the size of a coconut. Its roundness, perfect clarity, and marvelous sheen made it a jewel of incalculable value.

CCSs: RL.8.2, RL.8.10, RI.8.2, RI.8.3, RI.8.5

 TIP 2:   As soon as you finish reading, tell yourself what the passage is mostly about.

Sometimes the main idea of a passage is clearly stated, as in a headline that tells exactly what the article is about. Often, however, the main idea is suggested by the details of a piece of writing. It's up to you to put the pieces together to determine the main idea.

4.   Go back to the excerpt from *20,000 Leagues Under the Sea*. Underline any phrases or sentences that help describe what the passage is mainly about.

You probably won't be able to find one sentence that clearly tells the main idea of this passage. However, by identifying the important details and putting them together, you can come up with a pretty clear statement of the main idea on your own.

 TIP 3:   Main ideas can be stated or implied.

Sometimes the main idea of a passage is clearly stated, and sometimes it is left up to you to find it. An **explicit** main idea is clearly stated in the passage.

Often, however, you'll need to look a bit harder for the main idea. Sometimes, studying the details of a passage will help. **Details** are the bits and pieces of information that support the main idea or add interest to a passage. An **implied** main idea is suggested by the details of a piece of writing. When authors imply something, they don't come right out and say it. However, they leave enough clues in the details for readers to understand. In these passages, it's up to the reader to put the pieces together to determine the main idea. This is called making an inference. If an author implies a main idea, it is up to the reader to infer what it is. You'll learn more about making inferences in Lesson 3.

 TIP 4:   Find the answer choice that most closely matches your own statement of the main idea.

Just like your friend Herman, main idea questions ask, "What's it about?" One way to answer a main idea question is to imagine a friend has just asked you what a passage is about. If you can answer that question, you'll have found the main idea.

5.   Write one or two sentences that tell a friend what the excerpt from *20,000 Leagues Under the Sea* is mostly about.

_____

_____

_____

Remember, you need to include enough information to let someone else really know what's in the passage. If you had told Herman that "My First Goose" was "a really cool army story," he still wouldn't know much about the story. Make sure your statement of the main idea adequately describes the passage.

When answering multiple-choice questions about main idea on a test, compare your own statement of the main idea to the answer choices. The choice that most closely matches your statement is probably correct.

Look at the following answer choices, and compare them to your response to Number 5. Choose the sentence that is the best statement of the main idea.

6. What is the main idea of this passage?

   A. An explorer observes curious sites in a beautiful underwater cave.

   B. A team of divers explores an underwater cave, led by their captain.

   C. A man is shown a very valuable oyster hidden in an underwater cave.

   D. Captain Nemo pays a visit to a giant oyster and pearl he keeps hidden.

 TIP 5: Be aware that some answer choices are only details from the passage.

The main idea isn't just a detail from one part of the passage. It's what the passage as a whole is about.

Look at Number 6 again. Notice that no answer choice is completely false. Each describes something that happens in the passage. The trick is to figure out which choices are only details from the passage and which one describes the passage as a whole.

7. Look at the answer choices for Number 6 again, then skim the passage to find out where each is mentioned. Which of the answer choices are only details from the passage?

_____

_____

CCSs: RL.8.2, RI.8.2, RI.8.5

 TIP 6: Connect details to the main idea to determine which details are most important.

The most important details are those that strongly support the main idea. Ask yourself which details best support the main idea. These are the details you should pay closest attention to as you read.

8. What makes the narrator think that Captain Nemo has been in the cave before?

_____

_____

_____

9. Which of the following details supports the idea that Captain Nemo is keeping the oyster secret for a reason?

   A. The cave is hard to find.

   B. Nemo knows how to open the oyster.

   C. The oyster contains a large pearl.

   D. Nemo has visited the oyster before.

 TIP 7: Locate details in the passage by scanning for key words.

If you didn't pick up the answer to a detail question while you were reading, you must go back and find it in the passage. There's no need to reread the entire passage every time you encounter a detail question. Instead, you can simply look for key words and phrases related to the detail. This is called scanning. When you **scan** you run your eyes over the passage to look for a specific word or phrase.

10. Read the question below. Circle any key words and phrases in the question that might help you find the answer in the passage.

    What makes the narrator think the hidden pearl has "incalculable value"?

11. Scan the passage for the key words you circled in the previous question. When you find them, underline them. Then, reread the sentences in which the key words appear. Now answer question 12.

12. What makes the narrator think the hidden pearl has "incalculable value"?

    A. The oyster hiding the pearl is hard to open.

    B. The cave is dark and difficult to maneuver in.

    C. The pearl is a large, high-quality jewel.

    D. The captain has kept the pearl hidden for years.

 TIP 8: Make sure that your written summary includes all of the most important parts of the passage.

You may be asked to write a summary of your own. A good summary will include all of the most important parts of the passage: the major ideas and important details used to support those ideas. If the passage is a fictional story, the summary will include the main characters, the setting, and the most important events.

13. Summarize the excerpt from *20,000 Leagues Under the Sea* in your own words on the following lines.

    _____

    _____

    _____

    _____

    _____

Lesson Practice begins on the following page.

Directions: This passage is about life on a submarine. Read the passage. Then answer Numbers 1 through 5.

Life at Sea

by Levi Davis

Hayes had dreamed about this for as long as he could remember, and part of him couldn't believe it was actually happening. He was on a submarine in the middle of the ocean, and no amount of dreaming or training could have prepared him for it.

As a little boy, Hayes had been fascinated with ships and the water; specifically with submarines. His parents had encouraged his interest, first buying him plastic boats for the bathtub, and then, as he got older, finding him books on the history and capabilities of civil and military submarines. They'd even gone as far as visiting the Maritime Museum in San Diego when Hayes was in junior high. It had taken them two years to save for the trip. There, Hayes had toured the *USS Dolphin* and a B-39 sub, both of which he'd read about in his books. The *Dolphin* was the deepest diving submarine in the world, but it was the larger, less sleek B-39 that really held his interest. The B-39 had been a Soviet sub, the same kind that had actually been used to track U.S. and NATO ships during the Cold War. As he walked through the sub and listened to their tour guide, Hayes couldn't help but imagine the Soviet soldiers who had once stood in the same place, who had steered this very ship through enemy waters, tracking the U.S. counterparts meant to protect his own country. He'd been overwhelmed after the museum trip. Not by the size of the vessels or the close quarters of the subs, but by man's ability to imagine something so odd and powerful into being. That was the day Hayes decided to join the Navy.

Fifteen years later, he was nearing the end of his first full week on the *USS San Juan*. He sat down after a 6-hour work shift and tried to compose a letter to his parents. He wouldn't be able to put the letter in the mail until they made port in a few weeks, but he wanted to get his thoughts down just the same.

> Dear Mom and Dad,
>
> One week down; three months to go. I'm not allowed to tell you where we are or how deep we've gone, but I want you to rest assured that our current mission holds very little danger. I'd tell you that it's completely safe, but nothing ever is, right? Try not to worry. (Mom, I'm looking at you!) I thought you might like to know what life on a submarine is really like—in a way it's exactly what I imagined it would be all those years ago, but books are no substitute for reality.

You know the general workings of the sub and my place on it: it's 320 feet long and a little over 30 feet wide. It seems large when I write it like that, but cram a bunch of guys in a metal tube with no windows and it gets pretty small pretty fast. Even though I've only been here a week, I've already learned that I have to trust these guys completely. Not only with my life, but with my sanity. There's a reason submariners have to go through so many mental tests before they're allowed on a boat—I can't imagine how stressful this would be for someone who is claustrophobic. He'd be driven crazy, and make the rest of us crazy in the process.

So, my typical day: first of all, our days are 18 hours long instead of 24. We're divided into 3 watch sections, and each section is on duty for 6 hours and then off for 12. So I spend 6 hours every day working (wish I could tell you exactly what I'm doing, but I can't!), and then I have 12 hours of free time. Free time on a sub isn't exactly the same as it is on land, but we actually do a lot of the same things. There's athletic equipment so we can stay in shape; we play cards, eat, train, do regular maintenance. We can't exactly zip to the movie theater on a night off, but we brought along 400 movies so we're not lacking for entertainment. I eat four times a day: breakfast, lunch, dinner, and midnight rations (we call them "midrats"). The food's actually pretty good—our cook has entered contests with other Navy cooks and actually won, so don't worry about me having to eat prepackaged astronaut food or anything like that. We have the same stuff I had at home: eggs, pancakes, and cereal for breakfast; sandwiches and burgers for lunch; pasta and steak for dinner; and leftovers for midrats. Good thing there's a gym on board to work off all those calories. The only thing I really miss is seeing the sunrise and sunset. For us, those things don't exist, and I'll be thrilled to dock and see them again. On the other hand, I've never been as close to another group of people as I am to the men on board with me. You know I always wanted a brother; now I have hundreds.

What can I say? Life on a sub is both shockingly normal and kind of extraordinary. I hope you're both doing well. I just wanted to say thank you for everything you did to get me to this place, and I'll see you in three months!

Love,

Hayes

1. **Read the following sentence from the passage.**

   "Not by the size of the vessels or the close quarters of the subs, but by man's ability to imagine something so odd and powerful into being."

   What is the meaning of *quarters* as it is used in this passage?

   A. coins

   B. parts

   C. sections

   D. lodgings

2. **What is the main idea of paragraph 2?**

   A. Hayes went to the Maritime Museum in San Diego when he was young.

   B. Hayes' parents encouraged him by buying him toy boats and books about submarines.

   C. Hayes was meant to work on a submarine because he was fascinated by them his whole life.

   D. Hayes has a lot of free time to exercise and relax.

3. **What is the main idea of this passage?**

    _____

    _____

    _____

    _____

4. **Why does Hayes say that he trusts his shipmates with his sanity?**

    A.   The ship seems to be populated with crazy people.

    B.   The ship is so small that everyone must get along.

    C.   Hayes has met some interesting people in the Navy.

    D.   Hayes feels like his shipmates are basically his family.

5. **Write a summary of this passage. Remember to include the main idea and details from the passage in your response.**

    _____

    _____

    _____

    _____

    _____

Lesson 3: Reading Strategies

People usually choose their friends because they have something in common—they make a connection. Maybe they like the same kind of jokes. They might like the same kind of clothes, play the same sports, or enjoy the same type of music. Or, they might find that they think about things in the same way. Somehow, the friendship just makes sense.

This lesson is all about making connections. Sometimes, test questions will require you to understand the stated or implied connections between important details in a passage. You also will need to make a few logical connections on your own.

Read the following passage. It will be used to explain the tips in this lesson.

The Tale of the Sword in the Stone

Imagine a time centuries ago, when kings and queens ruled the lands of Europe, and knights served in the name of honor. England's King Uther died without a known heir, so the country went without a king for a number of years. Times were hard, and the people of England longed for a wise, noble ruler to lead them.

One day, a huge stone appeared outside a great cathedral in Londontown. An iron anvil[1] was set into the rock, and a gleaming sword stood half-buried in the anvil like a knife in an apple. Carved into the blade in large, friendly letters were these words:

> *Whosoever shall pull this Sword from this Stone*
> *is Rightful Heir to the Throne of England.*

The archbishop knew that every man in the kingdom would try his hand at drawing the sword if it meant a chance at the crown. So, the archbishop invited every noble in the kingdom to a New Year's Day tournament. There, knights would compete in games of skill and stamina. The winner, the archbishop hoped, would be the right man to draw the sword.

A young knight named Sir Kay came to take part in the tournament. Kay traveled to London with his father, Sir Ector, and a squire[2], Arthur, who had been raised as Kay's brother.

[1]**anvil:** a heavy iron block
[2]**squire:** a knight's assistant, who carries the knight's armor and weapons

When they arrived at the tournament, Kay realized that he had left his sword at the inn where they had passed the previous night. "Arthur," Kay said, "please return and fetch my weapon. I would go with ye, but I must stay rested for the competition."

Arthur agreed and dashed off through the cobblestone city streets. He hurried because he wanted to be of service to his master and brother. Arthur was not yet grown, so he was considered too young to compete in the tournament himself. Still, he did not want to miss any of the events. As the boy ran through the city, his mind drifted back to his meeting in the woods with the old man, Merlin. The wizard had shown Arthur a vision that promised greatness in his future.

The squire came upon the courtyard of the cathedral, which—unlike most days—was empty of people because of the tournament. He saw the sword sticking out of the stone. It didn't seem to belong to anyone, and Arthur was in a hurry to get back to the tournament. He jumped onto the stone and, with hardly a struggle, pulled the sword from the anvil. With a satisfied smile, Arthur wrapped the sword in his cloak and headed back to the tournament.

Arthur took the sword to Sir Kay, who did not recognize the weapon as his own. As he read the words on the blade, Kay slowly realized what he held: the key to rule all of England. Out of the corner of his eye, he glanced at Arthur, who was busily gathering the rest of Kay's armor for the contest. Kay ran to Sir Ector and exclaimed, "Father, I have the sword from the stone. I am the new king of England!"

Sir Ector saw through his son's boast. "Tell me, your majesty, how did ye come into possession of the sword?" He smiled, but his eyes were fierce.

Kay knew his father had caught him. "I cannot lie to you, Father. Arthur brought it to me."

Ector called Arthur before him and asked how he had come by this new sword. Arthur apologized. "I am sorry, Father, but Kay had left his sword at the inn, and instead of going back for it, I found this one. It was just sitting in a churchyard. I didn't think anyone wanted it."

"Did anyone see ye take it?" Ector asked.

"No," said Arthur. "Everyone was here, at the tournament."

"Return the sword, and we shall let everyone take a turn trying to pull it from the stone." Ector's command was gentle but definite, and Arthur did as he was told.

Ector told the archbishop that the sword had been drawn from the stone, and the archbishop immediately interrupted the tournament with the startling news. A great crowd had gathered by the time Arthur slipped the sword back into place in the anvil.

Arthur watched as the young knights lined up in the courtyard of the cathedral and each tried to pull the sword from the stone. All failed, including the brash Sir Kay.

Arthur now knew of the sword's importance and wondered if it could be true: Could he be the king? He had been raised by Sir Ector. The young squire had never known who his real parents were, and neither had Ector. Guided by the magician Merlin, Ector had raised the child in safety, far from the violent fights over who would be England's next king. Merlin had promised that one day a sign would appear that would lead the true king back to his rightful place.

At last, Arthur stepped up to the stone. It had been so easy the first time, when the young man had not understood the sword's significance. One more time he pulled, and again the shining blade slid out of the stone, flashing in the sunlight for all to see.

Sir Ector touched the young man's shoulder and pronounced his destiny. "We have found England's true and rightful king."

All the knights gathered around their chosen leader. "All hail Arthur," they cheered. "Long live the king!"

 TIP 1: **Pull together details from the passage to make inferences.**

As you learned in Lesson 2, to **infer** is to make an educated guess based on incomplete information. You use what you already know to figure something out.

Read the following question: *Why did Sir Ector raise Arthur?* Look for places in the passage where the author talks about Arthur's childhood. Then choose the correct answer below.

1. Why did Sir Ector raise Arthur?

    A. If it were known that Arthur was the heir to the throne, someone may have tried to kill him.

    B. Sir Ector did not have a son of his own, so he promised to take care of Arthur when Arthur's father died.

    C. Arthur was being trained in secret by the magician Merlin, who lived with Sir Ector.

    D. Arthur was being trained by Sir Ector to become a great knight so that he would know how to pull the sword from the stone.

2. Underline details in the passage that support your answer to Number 1.

Though the answers to inference questions won't be directly stated in the passage, they will be supported by the passage in some way—by the author's tone, by details in the passage, or by other clues. (You will learn more about author's tone in Lesson 4.) Always make sure your inferences are based on information in the passage.

TIP 2: Put together several details and inferences to draw conclusions.

Conclusions require you to connect several details and inferences to come up with a final understanding about a topic.

3. Which of the following conclusions is supported by the passage?

   A. Arthur is taking the throne in place of the rightful heir, Sir Kay.

   B. From the time he was a small child, Arthur was destined to become king.

   C. Arthur is able to pull the sword from the stone because he is the one who placed it there.

   D. Always knowing he would become king, Arthur has been waiting for his role to be revealed.

4. How do you know the answer to Number 3?

   _____

   _____

   _____

   _____

   _____

 TIP 3: A generalization can be applied broadly.

A **generalization** requires you to put together specific details to come up with a general statement or principle that can be applied to more than one situation. For example, based on his behavior, you might generalize that Sir Ector is wise. He is able to see through his son's false words, and he acts toward Arthur in ways that are honest and responsible. Based on what we know about him, we can guess that he is likely to act wisely in other situations, as well.

5. Which of the following is a valid generalization about medieval English society as shown in this story?

   A. Knights weren't allowed to become king because they were too violent.

   B. Citizens voted for their leaders every four years.

   C. Magicians made most of the people's decisions.

   D. People took mystical signs seriously.

CCSs: RL.8.1, RL.8.3, RI.8.1

6. Underline details in the passage that support your generalization in Number 5.

 TIP 4: Look for words that show a cause–and–effect relationship.

As you're reading a passage, you may come across words or phrases that signal a cause-and-effect relationship. Not all causes and effects are revealed by specific words, but looking for such words can be a good place to start.

Several words and phrases can tip you off to cause-and-effect relationships. Here are some examples.

because of	increased/decreased	so	therefore
resulted in	as a consequence of	hence	thus
in order to	was responsible for	led to	caused
in response to	due to	affected	since

7. Reread the first eight paragraphs of "The Tale of the Sword in the Stone." Underline any cause-and-effect words you see.

8. Why does the archbishop send a message to the knights and noblemen?

    A. to ask them to pray for a king for their land

    B. to ask them to watch Arthur pull the sword from the stone

    C. to ask them to help Sir Kay find the sword he had lost

    D. to ask them to compete in the New Year's Day celebrations

9. Why can't Arthur compete in the tournament?

    A. He is too busy trying to find Sir Kay's sword.

    B. Everyone knows he is really the king.

    C. He is on duty, serving Sir Kay.

    D. He is too young to compete.

TIP 5: Look for unstated cause–and–effect relationships.

Not all cause-and-effect relationships are described using the words listed in Tip 4. Often, it's up to the reader to make the connection. One way to do this is to create a *because* sentence that links two events.

To practice this tip, complete the following sentence:

10. Arthur first decides to pull the sword from the stone because

_____

Now use your sentence from Number 10 to answer Number 11.

11. Why does Arthur first decide to pull the sword from the stone?

   A. Merlin instructs him to take it.

   B. He cannot read the sign next to it.

   C. He is in a hurry to find a sword for Sir Kay.

   D. He wants to show that he is the true king.

TIP 6: Look for words that show a compare–and–contrast relationship.

Some words in the passage may signal when two things are being compared. Words such as *like*, *as*, *both*, *unlike*, and *but* can clue you in to logical relationships in which two things are shown to be alike or different. Pay attention to how these words are used when you encounter them in the passage.

Here's a list of several other words and phrases that can tip you off to a compare-and-contrast relationship.

Compare-and-Contrast Words

Similarities		Differences	
alike	like	but	instead
also	same	different	not
as well as	similar	even though	not like
both	together	except	though
just as	too	however	unlike

CCSs: RL.8.1, RL.8.3, RI.8.1

12. Reread the following paragraph from the passage. Underline any words that compare or contrast.

> The squire came upon the courtyard of the cathedral, which—unlike most days—was empty of people because of the tournament. He saw the sword sticking out of the stone. It didn't seem to belong to anyone, and Arthur was in a hurry to get back to the tournament. He jumped onto the stone and, with hardly a struggle, pulled the sword from the anvil. With a satisfied smile, Arthur wrapped the sword in his cloak and headed back to the tournament.

13. When Arthur first arrives, the courtyard of St. Paul's is different than usual in that it is

_____

 TIP 7: Make your own comparisons.

Not all comparisons will be signaled by the types of words listed in Tip 6. You may need to make some comparisons of your own.

14. Arthur and Sir Kay are alike in that they both _____

_____

_____

Making the Connections

There are many more techniques for examining and connecting the ideas in a passage. Here are just a few:

- **analysis** — separating a subject into its basic parts and looking closely at each
- **deduction** — using a general rule to understand a specific situation
- **induction** — adding up specific details to reach a general conclusion
- **synthesis** — combining elements from various sources to reach a general understanding

In some cases, you may need to make comparisons between two or more passages. When comparing two passages, notice how they are alike and different in the following areas:

- genre, or type of selection

- topic, main idea, and theme

- scope, or range of information about the topic

- quality and amount of supporting details

- characters, conflicts, and literary techniques

- organization

- author's tone, attitude, and purpose

Read the following passage. Then answer Numbers 15 through 17.

King Arthur: Man and Legend

by Alicia Monroe

Heroes often become legends over time, and in the case of Britain's King Arthur, stories of this "once and future king" have entertained audiences for more than a thousand years. Historians are vague about the real Arthur, but some of them believe he once existed. He may have lived in Southern Britain in the late 400s and early 500s and was able to unite his people to fight off Anglo-Saxon invaders who were occupying the island. The real Arthur was thought to have won many battles, but possibly died in a civil war at the battle of Camlann, around 537 CE. This was actually before the Middle Ages, so the real Arthur could not have been a medieval knight, as many believe. In this period, knights did not fight in suits of armor.

As generations passed, storytellers played up Arthur's achievements, creating a legend that includes a mysterious upbringing, a revelation of royalty with the sword in the stone, a magical adviser in Merlin, a round table of brave knights, and a beautiful queen. Even these basic details of the story are subject to different interpretations. Take, for instance, the round table. Was it an actual table in a round shape that was housed in Arthur's castle? Was this the place where Arthur's most trusted knights would gather? Or was it meant as a figure of speech for the knights themselves?

A monk, Geoffrey of Monmouth, put Arthur's story on paper in 1137, but there is evidence that the legend of Arthur was written about even before this time. There may have been poems or stories portraying Arthur as a warrior who defended Britain. No one knows if Geoffrey took his story from these previous versions or if he made it all up himself.

Sir Thomas Malory's *Le Morte d'Arthur* ("The Death of Arthur"), written in 1470, added to the legend and has become a famous work of classical fiction. Even though Geoffrey of Monmouth wrote about Arthur first, Malory's story has become the definitive version of the story. It was originally written in 8 books, but is currently published as 21 books. That's a lot of story for one man's legend!

Arthur continues to inspire novelists, playwrights, and filmmakers, and it seems his appeal will never die: that of a hero who saves the land, only to be betrayed by his queen and his most trusted knight.

15. The author of "King Arthur: Man and Legend" suggests that which event in the first passage did not actually happen?

    A. Arthur showing he is king by pulling a sword from a stone

    B. Arthur knowing an honorable knight named Sir Kay

    C. Arthur being raised from infancy by Sir Ector

    D. Arthur being crowned king of England

16. Compare "The Tale of the Sword and the Stone" with "King Arthur: Man and Legend." How do the passages differ in genre? In scope? In the author's attitude and purpose?

    _____

    _____

    _____

    _____

    _____

17. According to "King Arthur: Man and Legend," what can you infer about the real Arthur, if he actually existed?

    A. He was a respected and brave leader.

    B. He was surrounded by mysterious people.

    C. He was betrayed by those he loved most.

    D. He was the greatest king in history.

Lesson Practice begins on the following page.

Directions: These two passages are about a settlement called Acadia. Read the passages. Then answer Numbers 1 through 5.

The Great Upheaval

by Lee Addams

In the early 1600s, a group of French colonists settled in eastern Nova Scotia, in the country that is now known as Canada. The French called their settlement Acadia. Their version of the French language is still spoken, with some variation, in the Cajun region of Louisiana. This is because the Cajuns are descendents of the original Acadians, who were forced from Nova Scotia by the English in the mid-1700s.

By the 1700s, Acadia was in turmoil. France and Britain had been fighting over the territory for many years, and as a result, Acadians had grown mistrustful of government. Living in a disputed territory where the government was more concerned with gaining land than taking care of its people meant that the Acadians were neglected by those in power. Life wasn't easy, but the Acadians were a tight-knit and resourceful people. Since most of them had lived as peasants in France, they now lived as equals in Nova Scotia. There were no class divisions like there had been, and everyone had relatively the same degree of education. Most marriages were arranged. Love matches were rare, and required the consent of the bride's parents. There was a reason for this, though: the villagers had to take care of themselves, and as a result they were suspicious of outsiders. They often defied the authorities, whether the authorities were French or British.

In the mid 1700s, Acadia was under British rule. Britain had captured Acadia and all Acadians were forced to swear allegiance to Britain or to leave. Over the course of many years, as the French built a fort nearby and prepared for more fighting, the British grew nervous about the loyalty of the Acadian people. It all came to a head in 1755.

That summer, the British army attacked the French fort and burned many Acadian homes in the process. The Acadians who still refused to swear loyalty to Britain were expelled from Nova Scotia. This became known as the "Great Upheaval." Almost 7,000 Acadians were forced to leave, most going back to France or south to the United States. Of those heading to the U.S., many eventually settled in Louisiana. During the same time period, ownership of Louisiana transferred from France to Spain, and "Acadian" gradually became "Cajun."

The Story of Emmeline Labiche

by Sierra Kuthrap

Emmeline Labiche was raised in Acadia by her father. Her mother died when Emmeline was a young girl. A beautiful young woman, Emmeline became engaged to an equally fine young man, Louis Arceneaux. But in 1754, war between the British and the French was brewing.

Acadia had been controlled by the British for over forty years, and the British insisted that the French-speaking Acadians swear their loyalties to England. The Acadians refused, and the British forced thousands of Acadians to board ships heading south. Emmeline and Louis were torn asunder in the chaos. Many Acadians ended up in Louisiana, but Emmeline's family sailed to Maryland instead. And it was there Emmeline grew despondent, separated from the man she loved.

The young woman was not one to complain. She was a model daughter and a good citizen of her community. But she pined for Louis. She often took long walks in the countryside to be alone and to think of her lost love. Though she tried to hide her pain from her family, it became clear to all that Emmeline was overcome with a melancholy that left her quiet and reserved. Her father worried, but there was nothing to be done. After a few years of trying to make a new life, the family moved on. They decided to settle in Louisiana where they would be among their fellow Acadians.

Emmeline moved to this new place with a sense of calm acceptance. She did not complain but traveled in a cloak of sadness. Once she arrived in her new land, she continued her habit of taking walks, where she could think her thoughts and not be a bother to her loved ones. One evening, she came to a bayou where some young Acadians were working, and whom should she see but Louis Arceneaux!

She ran to her former fiancé, both happy and confused. When Louis saw his lost bride-to-be, he couldn't quite believe his eyes.

She reached out for him, saying, "Louis, it is I, Emmeline."

Tears came to Louis's eyes. "Oh, Emmeline, I am so sorry. When you and your family left, and my family came to the French bayou, I thought I had lost you forever. Now I am married to another woman. You must forget me."

Emmeline turned pale and backed away from Louis. Some say she fainted on the spot. After this, all remaining joy disappeared from Emmeline's life. She continued her solitary walks, talking to herself and dreaming about her past in Acadia. Eventually, she became ill from grief and passed away. Some say she can still be spotted along bayous, wandering the banks and picking wild flowers, a spirit of lost love and a tragic symbol of Acadian exile.

1. **Why were the Acadians forced from Nova Scotia?**

    A.   They lost a war with the French.

    B.   They wanted to move to the United States.

    C.   They could not afford to live in Canada.

    D.   They would not side with the British.

2. **Why did Acadians eventually become known as "Cajun"?**

    A.   "Cajun" was a Spanish term for the French settlers.

    B.   The Spanish government demanded they speak Spanish.

    C.   When they left Acadia, the people needed a new name.

    D.   "Cajun" was the name of the place where they settled.

3. **How is Emmeline's family different from Louis's family?**

    A.   Emmeline's family was unhappy living in Acadia.

    B.   Emmeline's family moved to Maryland after they left Acadia.

    C.   Emmeline's family did not approve of her engagement.

    D.   Emmeline's family refused to swear loyalty to England.

4. **Why is Emmeline confused when she first sees Louis?**

   A. She didn't expect to see him.

   B. She thought he was in Acadia.

   C. She can't believe he is married.

   D. She thinks he is someone else.

5. **How might have marriage to Louis been different for Emmeline than for most Acadian women? Use details from both passages and your own conclusions to support your answer.**

   _____

   _____

   _____

   _____

   _____

Lesson 4: Nonfiction

You arrive at school one day and find that a note has been dropped through the vents of your locker.

Dear Nyah,

    Please forgive me for what I said last night. You have beautiful hair, and I love your new haircut. I meant to say it was "charming" or "surprisingly chic" or something like that, but I couldn't think of the right words. "Dorky" just kind of popped out of my mouth. You know I think you're beautiful. I haven't been able to sleep all night thinking that I hurt your feelings. I'd do anything to patch things up.

                                       Your Friend,
                                       Josh

P.S. Hope this is the right locker. I'm so tired that they all look the same.

Before you toss the note into the recycling bin (who is Nyah, anyway?), you consider Josh's message. His tone is sincere. His attitude is concerned but positive. He obviously likes Nyah and is set on making amends. Just when you're ready to stuff the note into another locker, a sad-looking girl with surprisingly chic hair walks by. You hand her the note and say, "This is for you."

The Writer Behind the Writing

To understand a piece of writing, a reader frequently must understand some things about the person who wrote it. To do this, a reader must be able to spot clues about the author, the writer behind the writing.

In the case of the note above, you can judge that Josh is a sincere, if socially awkward, guy. What if he had written the note on the following page?

Dear Nyah,

When are you going to forgive me for what I said last night? So what if I said your new haircut looked dorky? I didn't mean it. The way you treated me really ticked me off. I couldn't even sleep last night. I mean, you know I'd never say anything to hurt you. Unless I was really really tired, like now. (Just kidding.)

Josh

If you had read this note, you'd be doing Nyah a favor to toss it in the nearest bin. This Josh could only be the evil twin of the one who wrote the first note. He's obviously an insincere, self-centered jerk.

The Author's Fingerprints

An author leaves his or her fingerprints all over a piece of writing. Several writers might be given the same assignment and each, amazingly, will produce something very different. This will happen no matter how simple the subject may seem.

You can uncover how an author feels about a topic by examining the choices he or she has made in creating the work. An author might select some details and reject others, or use big words and long sentences instead of short statements. Or an author might tell you a lot about himself or herself by saying something funny, or sad, or mean. Sometimes these verbal fingerprints are left behind intentionally, and sometimes they are not. Finding these fingerprints and analyzing them adds to the pleasure of reading.

Noticing an author's tone, attitude, and purpose can help you figure out a lot about an author. Information about these three things can be found by thinking about the choices an author has made, especially the words he or she has chosen to describe the facts in the passage.

TIP 1: The author's tone reveals his or her attitude toward a subject.

Author's **tone** is the attitude, or feeling, that the author has about the subject. The words and sentence structures authors use reveal their feelings about the topic they are writing about. When you read passages, imagine how the author would sound if he or she were speaking the words to you. Do the author's words convey approval or disapproval of the subject of the passage?

The author's tone in a passage can be positive, negative, or neutral.

- A **positive** tone conveys good feelings about the topic. It might show happiness, pride, delight, enthusiasm, humor, love, romance, or joy. The tone might be extremely positive or only slightly positive, depending upon the words the author chooses.

- A **negative** tone communicates bad feelings about the topic. It might show sadness, anger, cynicism, bitterness, weariness, hate, or disgust. Like a positive tone, word choice determines how negative the tone is.

- A **neutral** tone is neither positive nor negative. If an author has no opinion (or doesn't want to show one), he or she will avoid choosing words that express any sort of feeling at all. Words used to describe this tone include fair, straightforward, neutral, impartial, detached, and noncommittal.

All three of the following paragraphs describe the same experience, but each is written by a different author. Read each passage and answer the questions that follow.

Passage 1

I just saw this awesome new movie, *Space Heroes*! It's about this cool kid named Sam, who finds out that he's really an alien from Altair. An amazing starship, with brilliant flashing red and green lights, shoots out of the sky like a falling star and zips him back to his home planet, where he meets his handsome older brother, Zendar. Zendar flies a futuristic starfighter in a battle with some creepy green creatures. Needless to say, Sam and Zendar save the galaxy, and Sam falls in love with a beautiful alien girl called Mella. The special effects blew my mind, and the acting was great!

CCSs: RI.8.6, RI.8.8, RI.8.9

Passage 2

In the new film *Space Heroes*, a boy named Sam discovers he is not from Earth. A spaceship from his home planet arrives and takes Sam back to Altair. There Sam meets Zendar, who enlists him in a conflict with a rival alien race. An Altairian girl, Mella, serves as a love interest.

Passage 3

Hollywood has coughed up another chunk of garbage. *Space Heroes*, which should have been called *Space Zeros*, is a dull, formulaic exercise in special effects substituting for story. The main character, a blank-faced child named Sam, turns out to be an alien. We can tell because a clunky spaceship decorated in Christmas lights appears out of nowhere and drags the kid to another planet. No one on Earth seems to notice this. For some reason, Sam's "hunky" brother Zendar needs a thirteen-year-old kid with no experience to help him defend the planet Altair from some unconvincing green rubber bad guys. And because every lousy science-fiction movie needs a romantic subplot, there's a girl character named Mella who looks cute and gets rescued a lot. Unfortunately, no one saved her from being in this movie.

1. Describe the tone of Passage 1. Does it make you want to see the movie? Why or why not?

   _____

   _____

2. Describe the tone of Passage 2. Does it make you want to see the movie? Why or why not?

   _____

   _____

3. Describe the tone of Passage 3. Does it make you want to see the movie? Why or why not?

   _____

   _____

4. Underline words in Passage 3 that support your answer to Number 3.

5. Which phrase best describes the author's attitude toward the movie in Passage 1?

    A. slightly bored

    B. somewhat opposed

    C. somewhat approving

    D. very approving

6. What is the author's attitude toward the movie in Passage 3?

    A. curious

    B. hesitant

    C. critical

    D. undecided

 TIP 2: Pay close attention to the mood the author creates.

Mood is the general atmosphere the author creates. You can also think of mood as the feeling or emotion you get after reading a passage. Moods can be cheerful, spooky, suspicious, serious, and so on.

7. Which word best describes the mood the author creates in Passage 1?

    A. exciting

    B. joking

    C. serious

    D. frightening

CCSs: RI.8.6, RI.8.7

 TIP 3: Put it all together to determine the author's purpose.

The tone and mood, along with the details the author uses, will help you determine the **author's purpose**, or reason for writing. Authors have many different purposes for picking up their pens, but most fall into one of the categories in the chart below.

Purpose	Description	Examples
to inform	Authors share information without offering opinions. They may explain, describe, give facts, or otherwise inform you about a topic. They may also tell you how to do something.	news story in your daily newspaper, nonfiction article in a magazine, textbook, recipe, instructions
to entertain	Authors write texts with the readers' enjoyment in mind. They may seek to amuse readers with a funny story or essay, or frighten readers with a scary tale.	short story, novel, humorous essay, play, poem
to persuade	Sometimes authors want to convince you that their way of thinking is best. They might criticize something they don't like, warn of a future danger, or encourage you to take some action.	editorial, letter to the editor, review
to express	Authors may want to pour out their thoughts and feelings onto paper.	journal entry, poem, narrative

8. What is the author's purpose for writing Passage 2?

    A. to convince readers that a movie won't be any good

    B. to inform readers of basic details about a movie

    C. to persuade readers to go see a certain movie

    D. to entertain readers with a story about a space alien

Different Writers Write Differently

Almost any subject or topic can be written about in different ways. Just as no two people see things in exactly the same way, no two authors express ideas, themes, or issues in the same ways. When writers present you with facts, they select what they want you to know.

Reading more than one text about a topic is always a good idea. Comparing two or more viewpoints will give you a better understanding of the topic. It will also help you see some of the ways that authors can write about the same topic. You can even compare two passages from different genres.

TIP 4: **Recognize facts as statements that can be proven true or false.**

A **fact** is a statement that can be verified, or checked by asking experts, looking up information in a book, or direct observation. No matter how many people check it out, they'll all come up with the same information. Fact statements use words that have meanings everyone can agree on, such as *twenty*, *broken*, *yellow*, *water*, *millionaire*, *wildlife*, or *recycled*.

Fact statements can be correct or incorrect. For example, imagine that your friend Jordy says he spent the summer following the Lewis and Clark Trail across the Midwest, starting from Ohio and traveling through Illinois, Iowa, Nebraska, and Wyoming. Maybe you're not sure the trail that Lewis and Clark followed actually goes through each of those states, so you look on a map. According to the map, the Lewis and Clark trail does go through Ohio, Illinois, Iowa, and Nebraska, but then it heads north through Montana, rather than crossing Wyoming. You conclude that what Jordy had told you was a statement of fact, but his information was incorrect.

 TIP 5: **Recognize opinions as statements that describe feelings.**

A statement of opinion says, "This is what I believe to be true. I've thought about it and I've made up my mind." **Opinions** often use adjectives such as *joyous*, *talented*, *pitiful*, *junky*, *tasty*, *rich*, or *stinky*.

Opinions can change as easily as our moods. They vary from one person to another. A food that is delicious to your parents may be disgusting to you. You might find hundreds of people who share the same opinion about a topic—and who will argue heatedly that their opinion is right—but you're just as likely to find hundreds more who will disagree.

However, some opinions are stronger than others. **Informed opinions**, those that are based on knowledge and logic, are more useful than uninformed ones. For example, a physician is likely to hold a more valid opinion about a patient's condition than someone who has no medical training. Remember, everyone is entitled to his or her opinion, but that does not make all opinions equal.

As you work on the practice activity on the next page, keep in mind that facts can be checked, while opinions say what one person or group of people believes to be true.

CCSs: RI.8.4, RI.8.8, L.8.5a

 Practice Activity

Directions: Write "F" for Fact or "O" for Opinion in front of each statement.

_____ 1. George W. Ferris built the first Ferris wheel for the 1893 World's Fair.

_____ 2. The woods behind Taylor High are an ideal area for bird watching.

_____ 3. Ten thousand years ago, the United States was home to mammoths, mastodons, and giant sloths.

_____ 4. In California, it is actually illegal to ride a bicycle in a swimming pool.

_____ 5. When it comes to golf, Spring County has it all.

_____ 6. A visit to the aquarium is an unforgettable adventure.

_____ 7. Fly fishing is the single most relaxing way to spend a Saturday afternoon.

_____ 8. Camels can survive for several weeks without drinking water.

_____ 9. Yellowstone National Park encompasses more land than any other national park in the country.

_____10. Abraham Lincoln was 21 years old and barefoot when he made his very first public speech.

 TIP 6: Notice the writer's use of figurative language.

Figurative language is language that draws comparisons between two things. For example, if you were to say, "I'm so hungry I could eat a horse," what you really want is a large quantity of food, not an actual horse. You would be speaking figuratively.

Writers often aim for fresh, original, and even unusual comparisons using figurative language. They can use it for all kinds of writing, including stories, poetry, and nonfiction. A few of the most common types of figurative language are described on the next page.

A **metaphor** compares two things by saying (or suggesting) that one thing is another.

> Music is Lauren's lifeblood; she must have a daily infusion of rock, pop, rap, and jazz.

This sentence doesn't have anything to do with real blood. It means that music is as important to Lauren as her blood is. Lauren loves music so much that she needs to listen to it every day.

A **simile** compares two things using *like* or *as*.

> When my sister is in a bad mood, her bedroom is like a monster's lair: those who enter are lucky to make it out alive.

Again, this sentence shouldn't be taken literally. It is another way of saying that the writer's sister is very mean when she's angry and it's best to avoid her.

An **allusion** is a reference a writer makes to a familiar person, place, or event.

> Lucia felt like Cinderella five minutes before midnight.

Here, the writer is referring to a well-known fairy tale. Most readers know that Cinderella is a poor girl who has an exciting opportunity to go to a ball and meet a prince. However, her good fortune ends at midnight. The writer uses this allusion to show the reader that like Cinderella, Lucia felt wonderful, but she knew the good feeling wasn't going to last long.

Now write your own examples of figurative language.

9. metaphor _____

_____

10. simile _____

_____

11. allusion _____

_____

CCSs: RI.8.7, RI.8.8

 TIP 7: Judge the validity of the writing.

Finally, go back over all the factors you have considered and determine how well the author has composed his or her work. Is the tone appropriate? Does the mood help convey the main idea? Does the author present a logical argument without assuming you already agree with some of his or her ideas? Does the author's style make the writing enjoyable to read? Did the author use the form of writing that best represents his or her ideas?

If you can answer the above questions and others in positive ways, then the author is doing his or her job. You don't have to agree with what an author says to appreciate effective writing. On the other hand, if an author seems unable to write clearly and logically, you probably won't agree with him or her anyway.

Lesson Practice begins on the following page.

Directions: These passages are about the green movement. Read the passages. Then answer Numbers 1 through 6.

Think Before You Act

by Jessie Sinclair

There's been a lot of discussion lately about how we can "go green." I'm all for a cleaner planet, but it seems that the younger generation is gung-ho on forcing unreasonable changes on the rest of us. What they are asking us to do is sometimes expensive and often inconvenient. Everyone is just turning "green" because it's so cool. Just because certain celebrities have embraced the movement, young people think they should, too. There is no real commitment, just a lot of hype.

While we appreciate their enthusiasm, some of us resent being asked to go along with these idealistic schemes. For example, I don't think I should have to buy all these new low-energy light bulbs. Those aren't cheap! The newest thing is to avoid using the dryer or dishwasher whenever possible. Now, who do you think hangs the clothes out to dry instead of putting them in the dryer? It's usually the parent who ends up in the hot sun, doing what a machine could do in half the time. Why don't some of these kids forgo playing video games for fifteen minutes to hang the laundry out?

As if that weren't enough, now we're being asked to cut back on driving. Our communities are built for driving, not walking or biking. We can't change that. Everyone else is driving all they want, so why shouldn't we? Environmentalists want to force everyone to carpool. I say, let them take the bus and let us drive in peace. It's not as if the tiny amount of gas we would save each week by carpooling would make a big dent in the energy problem.

To top it all off, none of these changes is even necessary. Paul Luter, the president of Best Fossil Fuels Inc., says that there is no need to worry; his company has just done a study stating that finding alternative energy sources is costly and premature.

In closing, I just want to tell all of the spoiled brat environmentalists to back off and let their parents make the decisions about the family's energy usage. They'll learn soon enough they can't save the world alone.

No More Excuses

by Cedric Collins

There are no more excuses, people. The movement to go green can no longer be considered just a fad; it is now a necessary and legitimate way of life. There are those who think the green movement, and environmentalism as a whole, is nonsense, a recent trend that means little. But the truth is, the roots of environmentalism go back much further than the last couple of decades. Henry David Thoreau pushed for conservation way back in the 1800s. Not everyone needs to move out into the woods and do away with modern conveniences, but we should at least be educated. The whole world needs to get on board with conservation or we risk losing everything. And while that might sound scary (and it is), the truth is, we need to rely on facts, not emotions.

Here's what we know: More than half of the world's tropical forests have been lost. Half! These forests take thousands of years to grow and are destroyed in a matter of minutes. Trees not only provide us with clean oxygen, but great advances in medicine have been discovered in rain forests. The National Cancer Institute has identified over 3,000 plants that can be used in the fight against cancer, and 70% of these plants are found in the rain forest. Just imagine what is still out there just waiting to be discovered. Would you really risk the rest of the world's rain forests when they could hold a possible cure for cancer?

Animals are becoming extinct at an alarming rate. If current trends continue, estimates show that 1/3 of all animal species on the planet may be extinct by 2100. The animal kingdom survives as species hunt and feed off of one another, keeping everything in balance. What happens when the balance is upset?

These are relatively big issues, but there are smaller things you can do every day to help the environment.

It takes 450 years for a plastic bottle to decompose, meaning that bottle of water you picked up at the supermarket today is going to be around for a lot longer than you are. Think 450 years is too long to comprehend? Imagine the founding fathers had been drinking out of plastic water bottles when they signed the Declaration of Independence. Parts of those bottles would still be around today.

Did you know that a simple leaky faucet wastes 13 liters of water a day? That's almost 1,254 gallons a year, simply because you have a drip in the bathroom sink. Every ton of recycled paper saves 380 gallons of oil. Using energy-efficient lightbulbs instead of standard 75-watt bulbs can prevent the release of one ton of carbon dioxide into the atmosphere.

The world population is estimated at almost 7 billion today. By 2050, there will be more than 9 billion people on this planet. Now's the time to take hold of our own destinies and erase some of the damage we've done to our home. It's our only one, and it's not too late.

1. **What is the author's purpose in writing "Think Before You Act"?**

   A. He is trying to entertain readers with a funny story about teenage environmentalists.

   B. He wants to convince readers to leave environmental decisions to their parents.

   C. He wants to inform readers about the things they can do to help the environment.

   D. He is trying to explain why there is no reason to panic about the environment.

2. **Which of these best describes the mood of "Think Before You Act"?**

   A. cheerful

   B. annoyed

   C. serious

   D. suspicious

3. **What is the author's purpose in writing "No More Excuses"?**

   A. He wants people to recognize the work of Henry David Thoreau.

   B. He is trying to show the rich and detailed history of environmentalism.

   C. He wants people to know what will happen if we ignore the environment.

   D. He is trying to convince readers to stop drinking out of plastic bottles.

4. **Which of these best describes the mood of "No More Excuses"?**

   A. humorous

   B. angry

   C. frightened

   D. serious

62 | Practice

5. Compare the authors' tones. How are their attitudes toward conservation and environmentalism different? Use details from both of the passages and your own conclusions to support your answer.

    _____

    _____

    _____

    _____

6. Imagine that you know nothing about the green movement. Which of these passages would be more likely to persuade you? Why? Use details from both passages and your own conclusions to support your answer.

    _____

    _____

    _____

    _____

Lesson 5: Stories and Drama

Imagine that 10 different authors were gathered in a room and told to write on the topic of courage. One author might choose to write a story about police officers chasing dangerous criminals. Another might write a biography about a brave person in history. There are many different ways to tell the same story. In this lesson you'll learn more about the different reading genres and how to recognize the elements used in each.

 TIP 1: Figure out what type of writing the passage is.

A **genre** is a type, or category, of written work. There are many genres. Often, knowing the genre of a passage can help you know what to expect and help you to better understand the passage.

Different genres are put together in different ways. For example, a science-fiction story about Mars and a nonfiction piece about the Mars Pathfinder mission unfold differently. Each will "feel" different from the other as you read it.

The four major genres are fiction, nonfiction, drama, and poetry.

- **Fiction** tells a made-up story. Fiction often comes in the form of a short story or novel. There are many types of fiction: horror, mystery, fantasy, adventure, historical fiction, science fiction, fables, and folktales, to name a few.

- **Nonfiction** passages tell about real-life people, places, things, ideas, or events. Types of nonfiction include biography, autobiography, informative articles, opinion pieces, instructions, letters to the editor, and so on. Well-written works of nonfiction can be as entertaining as good fiction, but nonfiction works tend to be factual.

- **Drama** is the genre in which "the play's the thing." A play is written to be performed on stage. It tells the actors which lines to speak, as well as where and how to move on stage. Shakespeare's *Romeo and Juliet* is one example of a play.

- **Poetry** comes in all styles, shapes, and sizes. Some poems tell a story; others simply describe an image. Some rhyme; others don't. Most poems try to express ideas and feelings in unusual ways, often using figurative language.

CCSs: RL.8.3, RL.8.10

1. Complete the chart by writing the title of one work you have read in each genre.

Genre	Example
fiction	
nonfiction	
drama	
poetry	

You already understand a lot about story types and structures. When you were learning to talk, you picked up the basic patterns of speech because you heard them all the time. In the same way, you've picked up the basic patterns of stories after hearing and reading so many of them. Read the following paragraphs. Each paragraph is the beginning of a different story.

Story 1

It was a dark and stormy night. Inside the Victorian house her family had just moved into, Julie sat on a crushed-velvet sofa and stroked her nervous cat. "Well, it's a dark and stormy night," Julie mumbled. "I guess we'll find out just what kind of protection this house has to offer." A sudden flash of lightning, followed by thunder, caused her to add, in a trembling voice, "Won't we, Sissy?" The cat responded with a long, drawn-out growl, her tail swishing wildly from one side to the other.

Story 2

Once upon a time, long, long ago, along the edge of a fertile valley leading to the sea, there lived a Viking lord and his family. Young men who had proven themselves in battle would come to the valley, hoping to make the lord's lovely daughter, Kristina, their bride. The lord and his wife made great shows of hospitality. But Kristina would take one look at her suitors and retire silently to her chamber. None of them matched the handsome man she had seen in that startling dream two years ago.

Story 3

The police reached the crime scene at 4:00 AM to find broken glass strewn everywhere. Arriving just forty-five minutes later, Detective Dick Stevens was a little gruff: Not only had his sleep been interrupted, but his morning training schedule would be thrown out of whack. The marathon was only thirteen days away.

Write one sentence telling what you think will happen in each story.

2. Story 1 _____

_____

3. Story 2 _____

_____

4. Story 3 _____

_____

In this lesson, you will learn about the basic elements found in almost all stories: character, setting, and plot. You will look at the way an author tells a story—the choices he or she makes that create style, tone, mood, and meaning, just as they do in nonfiction.

Fiction Forms

Looking for a good story? Fiction stories can be found in many different forms.

- **short story**—a brief story with few characters with one central problem

- **novel**—longer and more complex than a short story, with characters and events described in great detail

- **novella**—a piece of fiction that falls between a short story and a novel in length and complexity

- **anthology**—a collection of writings, often by many different authors

TIP 2: Keep in mind the characteristics of fiction subgenres.

Part of knowing how these stories will develop depends on knowing the basic types, or subgenres, of fiction. Here are just a few of them.

Fiction Subgenre	Traits
action adventure	A story featuring one action-packed scene after another. What it lacks in characterization, it makes up for in plot.
contemporary fiction	A story that takes place in the present day or recent past, in a society similar to our own.
fairy tale	A traditional story with familiar character types, such as a hero and a villain, that usually has a happy ending.
fantasy	A story with one or more features that are not seen in our world, such as magic, time travel, or talking animals.
folktale	A traditional story handed down from generation to generation by word of mouth. Fables, tall tales, myths, legends, and fairy tales may be considered folktales.
historical fiction	A story set during a specific time in history. It may include actual historical figures or events, but the plot, characterization, and dialogue is mostly made up by the author.
mystery	A story in which a crime is committed. A character in the story must unravel a web of clues before pinning down the suspect.
realistic fiction	A believable story that could happen to the reader. The main character often faces an emotional or a psychological conflict.
science fiction	A type of fantasy story set in a time or place in which technology has reshaped society in significant ways.

Story 1 on page 65 is a scary story designed to raise the hair on your arms. Story 2 is a fairy tale, so you can guess that Kristina will eventually meet the "man of her dreams." Story 3 is from a mystery. You know that Detective Dick Stevens will find the criminal and run the marathon and that, somehow, those two things will be connected.

TIP 3: **Recognize the "building blocks" of storytelling: plot, character, and setting.**

Most stories boil down to this statement: Something happens to someone, somewhere. The "something" that happens is called the **plot** of the story. The "someone" to whom it happens (or who makes it happen) is a **character**. The "somewhere" is the **setting**, where and when the story takes place.

Read the following story. It will be used to help you understand the tips in this lesson.

from

The Emerald City of Oz

by L. Frank Baum

It was a beautiful evening, so they drew their camp chairs in a circle before one of the tents and began to tell stories to amuse themselves and pass away the time before they went to bed.

Pretty soon a zebra was seen coming out of the forest, and he trotted straight up to them and said politely:

"Good evening, people."

The zebra was a sleek little animal and had a slender head, a stubby mane and a paint-brush tail—very like a donkey's. His neatly shaped white body was covered with regular bars of dark brown, and his hoofs were delicate as those of a deer.

"Good evening, friend Zebra," said Omby Amby, in reply to the creature's greeting. "Can we do anything for you?"

"Yes," answered the zebra. "I should like you to settle a dispute that has long been a bother to me, as to whether there is more water or land in the world."

"Who are you disputing with?" asked the Wizard.

"With a soft-shell crab," said the zebra. "He lives in a pool where I go to drink every day, and he is a very impertinent crab, I assure you. I have told him many times that the land is much greater in extent than the water, but he will not be convinced. Even this very evening, when I told him he was an insignificant creature who lived in a small pool, he asserted that the water was greater and more important than the land. So, seeing your camp, I decided to ask you to settle the dispute for once and all, that I may not be further annoyed by this ignorant crab."

CCSs: RL.8.3, RL.8.6

 TIP 4: Get to know the characters through what they say and do.

We already have a sense of the main characters in this excerpt. The zebra has approached Dorothy's group for help, but he also describes the crab as "impertinent," "insignificant," and "ignorant." What kind of character is polite on the outside yet uses words like this to describe someone who is not there to defend himself? The zebra's tone might be friendly, but his words are anything but.

5. Which word best describes Omby Amby?

    A. rude

    B. serious

    C. enthusiastic

    D. understanding

6. Which word best describes the zebra?

    A. furious

    B. dishonest

    C. irritated

    D. disapproving

Character Clues

Here are some questions to ask yourself about each character in a story:

• Is this a major or minor character?

• What is the character like?

• What does the character want most? Why?

• What is the main problem the character faces?

• How does the character view his or her situation?

• What kinds of relationships does he or she have with other characters in the story?

• How do the interactions of the characters affect the plot?

• How does the character change during the story?

One way in which authors create effective stories is by using well-developed characters. These characters are called **round**, or "three-dimensional," because the author has described them so well that they seem like real people. Round characters make us care about what happens in a story and want to read on. If you have ever felt as though the characters in a book were your friends, you know how important round characters are to a story. Less-developed characters are called **flat** characters. Minor characters who are not very important to the story may be described in a few words and may show only a limited range of emotions.

You have already begun to get an idea of what the main characters of "The Emerald City of Oz" are like. You might also expect that these characters will change in some way by the end of the tale. After all, change is what makes stories (and the people in them) interesting. Characters who undergo changes in a story are called **dynamic characters**. A dynamic character might gain new ideas, learn an important lesson, or form a different opinion about something or someone. By the end of a story, dynamic characters will be different, somehow, from how they once were. Characters who do *not* change throughout a story are called **static characters**. Usually, the main characters are dynamic, and the minor characters are static.

7. Based on what you have read so far in "The Emerald City of Oz," who is most likely to be a dynamic character? Why?

_____

_____

_____

_____

 TIP 5: Look for details that describe the setting.

The setting of a story includes not only the physical location, but also the time of day, time of year, point in history, weather, landscape, and so on. All of these things can contribute to your understanding of a story. An author often will sprinkle details throughout a story to describe the setting.

8. Go back to the passage and underline details that describe the setting of "The Emerald City of Oz."

9. The setting of the passage includes all of the following except

    A. evening.

    B. tents.

    C. a forest.

    D. a farm.

 TIP 6: Notice how the setting affects mood, tone, and meaning.

When you begin reading a story, your mind enters into the world created by the author. The way the setting makes you feel contributes to the mood in the story. As you learned in Lesson 4, **mood** is the general atmosphere of the story, the overall feeling the story creates in the reader. The mood can be gloomy, scary, funny, romantic, adventurous, and so on.

Tone shows the narrator's attitude toward the subject through his or her word choice. Just as in nonfiction, a fiction writer's tone can be sarcastic, serious, ironic, cheerful, hesitant, angry, and so on.

Setting can also have a strong effect on the meaning of the story. The historical events during a certain time period, or the customs of a particular place, may help define what the story is about. For example, there are many stories about young people becoming adults, but this change may happen in very different ways, depending on the setting.

10. The main setting of "The Emerald City of Oz" is next to a campfire in a land where animals can talk. Based on the setting, what is the mood of the story?

    A. bleak

    B. gloomy

    C. threatening

    D. lighthearted

What Would Huck Do?

To better understand how the setting affects the characters and the story, think about a similar situation from another story, and remember how that story's characters solved their problems. Characters living in a certain time and place are able to act based only on what they know and what is possible in their setting. For example, Huckleberry Finn might sail a raft down a river to escape his troubles; Bart Simpson would take a skateboard; Princess Leia would use a starship. Characters from different times and places may find themselves in similar situations, but their solutions are related to the time and place in which they exist.

TIP 7: Find the conflict in a story to understand the plot.

Aristotle, a philosopher who lived in ancient Greece, described the essence of fiction as "beginning, middle, and end." Things change over the course of a story; your initial judgments may be reversed as the plot thickens. The diagram to the right shows the basic plot structure used in most stories.

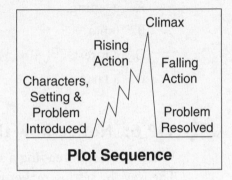

Most plots in fiction develop out of conflict. The main character in a story might be in conflict with another person, society, nature, or himself/herself. He or she may have to overcome a basic problem, such as a fear of flying or a lost homework assignment. The plot of a story will develop and eventually resolve these conflicts.

11. So far, what is the basic conflict of this passage from "The Emerald City of Oz"?

    A. There are not enough tents for everyone.

    B. A zebra is lost in a forest.

    C. A zebra has a disagreement with a crab.

    D. Dorothy is lost in the Land of Oz.

As you continue reading "The Emerald City of Oz," notice how the plot develops.

The Emerald City of Oz

(continued)

When they had listened to this explanation Dorothy inquired, "Where is the soft-shell crab?"

"Not far away," replied the zebra. "If you will agree to judge between us, I will run and get him."

"Run along, then," said the little girl.

So the animal pranced into the forest and soon came trotting back to them. When he drew near they found a soft-shell crab clinging fast to the stiff hair of the zebra's head, where it held on by one claw.

"Now then, Mr. Crab," said the zebra, "here are the people I told you about; and they know more than you do, who live in a pool, and more than I do, who live in a forest. For they have been travelers all over the world, and know every part of it."

"There's more of the world than Oz," declared the crab, in a stubborn voice.

"That is true," said Dorothy; "but I used to live in Kansas, in the United States, and I've been to California and to Australia—and so has Uncle Henry."

"For my part," added the Shaggy Man, "I've been to Mexico and Boston and many other foreign countries."

"And I," said the Wizard, "have been to Europe and Ireland."

"So you see," continued the zebra, addressing the crab, "here are people of real consequence, who know what they are talking about."

"Then they know there's more water in the world than there is land," asserted the crab, in a shrill, petulant voice.

"They know you are wrong to make such an absurd statement, and they will probably think you are a lobster instead of a crab," retorted the animal.

At this taunt the crab reached out its other claw and seized the zebra's ear, and the creature gave a cry of pain and began prancing up and down, trying to shake off the crab, which clung fast.

"Stop pinching!" cried the zebra. "You promised not to pinch if I would carry you here!"

"And you promised to treat me respectfully," said the crab, letting go of the ear.

"Well, haven't I?" demanded the zebra.

"No; you called me a lobster," said the crab.

"Ladies and gentlemen," continued the zebra, "please pardon my poor friend, because he is ignorant and stupid, and does not understand. Also the pinch of his claw is very annoying. So pray tell him that the world contains more land than water, and when he has heard your judgment I will carry him back and dump him into his pool, where I hope he will be more modest in the future."

"But we cannot tell him that," said Dorothy, gravely, "because it would not be true."

Now we have a fuller sense of the conflict between the zebra and the crab. As we see the characters interacting with one another, we are given a clearer picture of their relationship, and we understand how their personalities might have led them to this conflict.

As the story develops (the **rising action**), the character or characters will try to resolve the main conflict. Several complications, or smaller problems, usually need to be solved along the way. Eventually, the characters will find a solution to the main problem or else accept that there is no solution. The high point of the story, when the main problem must be faced once and for all, is called the **climax** (the climax is also sometimes called the "turning point").

The **falling action** leads to the **resolution** of the conflict. A resolution doesn't necessarily mean the problem has been solved. Rather, it describes or explains the outcome of the action and often points to the theme—the message or lesson—of the story.

12. Which of the following is a complication in the plot of "The Emerald City of Oz"?

    A. The zebra cannot find the crab.

    B. The zebra and the crab begin to fight.

    C. The crab refuses to listen to the campers.

    D. The crab falls off the zebra and is hurt.

13. How do you predict the conflict in "The Emerald City of Oz" will be resolved?

    _____

    _____

    _____

    _____

CCSs: RL.8.3, RL.8.10

Now you will read the next part of the story to see if your prediction is correct.

The Emerald City of Oz

(continued)

"What!" exclaimed the zebra, in astonishment. "Do I hear you alright?"

"The soft-shell crab is correct," declared the Wizard. "There is considerably more water than there is land in the world."

"Impossible!" protested the zebra. "Why, I can run for days upon the land, and find but little water."

"Did you ever see an ocean?" asked Dorothy.

"Never," admitted the zebra. "There is no such thing as an ocean in the Land of Oz."

"Well, there are several oceans in the world," said Dorothy, "and people sail ships upon these oceans for weeks and weeks and never see a bit of land at all. And geography will tell you that all the oceans put together are bigger than all the land put together."

At this the crab began laughing in queer chuckles that reminded Dorothy of the way Billina sometimes cackled.

"Now will you give up, Mr. Zebra?" it cried, jeeringly. "Now will you give up?"

The zebra seemed much humbled.

14. Which of the following is part of the climax of the story?

    A. The Wizard tells the zebra there is more water on Earth than on land.

    B. The zebra says it's impossible for there to be more water on Earth.

    C. The crab pinches the zebra's ear.

    D. The zebra calls the crab ignorant and stupid.

15. How is the conflict resolved in the story?

    _____

    _____

    _____

    _____

TIP 8: Identify who is telling the story.

Character, setting, and plot are the backbone of fiction. **Point of view**, the perspective from which the story is told, is another basic element, determining how much we get to know about the characters and the plot.

Every story has a **narrator**, the person who tells the story. If the narrator is a character in the story, the story is told in the first person. **First-person narrators** refer to themselves by using pronouns such as *I*, *me*, *myself*, *we*, and *our*.

A story with a **second-person** point of view is written as though the reader is the main character ("You wake up and brush your teeth"). Choose-your-own-adventure stories and directions are written in the second person.

The narrator can also be like an invisible observer who is not a character in the story, but who sees and hears everything that takes place. This point of view is called **third-person omniscient**. (*Omniscient* means "all-knowing"). A narrator can also be an invisible outsider able to describe the thoughts of only *one* of the characters. This point of view is called **third-person limited**. Third-person narrators generally do not mention themselves at all.

You should be able to "hear" the narrator through the story's voice. What words does this person use? Is the language very formal, or does it contain a lot of slang? Does the story sound like it's being told by a college professor, or by the main character's ten-year-old neighbor? No matter who is telling the story, a strong voice helps to keep our interest.

16. Who is telling the story in "The Emerald City of Oz"?

   A. Dorothy

   B. the Wizard

   C. the zebra

   D. an outside observer

17. From which point of view is "The Emerald City of Oz" told?

   A. first person

   B. second person

   C. third-person omniscient

   D. third-person limited

CCSs: RL.8.3, RL.8.6, L.8.5a

 TIP 9: Look for examples of irony.

Irony is the contrast between what is expected and what actually happens. It is a tool writers can use to build suspense or humor and is often impacted by point of view. There are many types of irony, but some of the most common are verbal, situational, and dramatic irony. In each case, what is said or done is the reverse of what is expected.

For example, consider this situation: Sari crashes her bicycle and skins her knee. Her best friend, Chauncy, asks whether it stings. Chauncy expects Sari to report that her knee hurts, but instead, she sweetly says, "I can't imagine a more pleasant sensation." When Sari (or an author or character) says the opposite of what she means, she is using **verbal irony**.

Situational irony occurs when the reader or the characters expect one thing to happen, but the reverse occurs. For example, Sari decides to help her math teacher by erasing problems from today's class from the chalkboard. The next day Sari finds out that the teacher was going to use those problems again and had to rewrite them on the chalkboard. Sari expected the teacher to be grateful for her help, but instead she has only caused a problem.

Dramatic irony occurs when we—the audience—know more than the characters in a story. For that reason, what a character says and does has a different meaning for us than it does for him or her. One of the most famous examples of dramatic irony comes at the climax of William Shakespeare's play *Romeo and Juliet*. The audience knows that Juliet has taken a sleeping potion that makes her seem dead. When Romeo finds her, he believes she's really dead, and kills himself as a result. We experience dramatic irony as we watch him and think, "Don't do it, you fool—she's not really dead!"

18. Find an example of irony in "The Emerald City of Oz" and write it below. What type of irony is it?

_____

_____

_____

_____

TIP 10: Recognize the elements of drama.

As you know, drama is the genre of writing meant to be performed on stage. Drama doesn't necessarily mean the play has to be dramatic or filled with serious and heavy subject matter. Plays can be humorous or thought provoking, silly or serious. Like all other genres of fiction, drama contains characters, setting, and plot. However, each of these appears differently in a drama than it is in a story.

The setting of a play is often conveyed through the **set description**. Set description is exactly what it sounds like: a description of what the set (or stage) should look like. For example, for a performance of *Our Town*, the set description might call for a streetlamp to be placed in the forefront of the stage and town buildings to be painted near the back.

The plot and the characters are advanced through dialogue and stage direction. **Dialogue** encompasses all the words spoken by the actors. Dramas rely heavily on dialogue. The way an actor reads a line of dialogue—gleefully or restrained, mournfully or angrily—dictates the way the audience should feel about the character. Since the audience cannot read a descriptive paragraph about each character, we must learn about them from the words and actions taking place on stage.

Often, these are choices made by the actor or director of a play, but sometimes directions will be written into the play itself. These are called stage directions. The director of a play determines how closely to follow a playwright's **stage directions** exactly. One of Shakepseare's most famous stage directions, found in *The Winter's Tale*, says simply, "Exit, pursued by a bear." Directors have interpreted this many ways in the hundreds of years since the play was published. Some have interpreted it literally, using a person dressed in a bear costume to chase the character Antigonus off the stage and to his death. Others have attempted to follow the direction in a less literal way.

Part of "The Emerald City of Oz" has been recreated below as a drama. Read the excerpt and then answer Numbers 19 through 21.

<u>SCENE 1</u>

The curtain opens on a black backdrop with stars illuminated. Trees and shrubs represent a forest. Tents are arranged among them. At the center of the stage, a small group is gathered around a campfire. They are clearly friendly and are enjoying the company of one another. A conversation is already in progress.

OMBY AMBY: ...so after putting in all of this time memorizing the stolen act ... the jester wasn't aware that his arch-rival had been invited to perform as well!...

[*A zebra trots out of the forest and approaches the campfire.*]

ZEBRA: [*politely*] Good evening, people.

OMBY AMBY: Good evening, friend Zebra. Can we do anything for you?

ZEBRA: Yes. I should like you to settle a dispute that has long been a bother to me, as to whether there is more water or land in the world.

WIZARD: Who are you disputing with?

ZEBRA: With a soft-shell crab. He lives in a pool where I go to drink every day, and he is a very impertinent crab, I assure you. I have told him many times that the land is much greater in extent than the water, but he will not be convinced. Even this very evening, when I told him he was an insignificant creature who lived in a small pool, he asserted that the water was greater and more important than the land. So, seeing your camp, I decided to ask you to settle the dispute for once and all, that I may not be further annoyed by this ignorant crab.

DOROTHY: Where is the soft-shelled crab?

ZEBRA: Not far away. If you will agree to judge between us I will run and get him.

DOROTHY: Run along, then.

[*ZEBRA exits. Curtain closes.*]

19. The paragraph beginning "Scene 1" is an example of

    A. stage direction

    B. set description

    C. dialogue

    D. plot

20. There are not many stage directions in this excerpt that tell the actors how to read their lines. How might the play's tone change depending on how the actors choose to portray their characters?

    _____

    _____

    _____

    _____

21. How does this excerpt differ from the story on page 68 that featured the same scene? Which version gives the reader better clues as to characters' personalities?

    _____

    _____

    _____

    _____

Lesson Practice begins on the following page.

Directions: This passage is about a young waitress who learns an important lesson. Read the passage. Then answer Numbers 1 through 5.

The Mashed Potato Incident

by Annie Roberts

David was my boss at the Crooked Tree Café. Every day after the lunch rush, he would pour himself a cup of coffee, grab a piece of peach pie, sit down in a booth, and flip through the *Plain Dealer*. He'd read the comics, then the news. One day, David called me over after I'd finished my shift.

"Caroline, do you know how much it costs to dry-clean a linen suit?" he asked.

I guessed fifteen dollars.

"No," David said, "try thirty-nine dollars, forty cents. That's the exact amount. I know because that's how much I reimbursed Mr. Stevens. You might remember him better as Mashed Potato Pants."

I remembered. The guy was a grouchy businessman, the sort of person who snaps his fingers when he wants something instead of asking nicely. He'd demanded a grilled chicken breast, green beans, and mashed potatoes. This was the first summer I'd had a job, and I didn't quite have the hang of balancing things. I tried to carry a plate of food, a glass of iced tea, and a basket of rolls to the businessman's table. I tripped, and the plate landed—potato-side-down, of course—on the guy's suit. His face turned as red as a stop sign, and he shouted for the manager. That would be David.

"I can pay you back for the cleaning bill," I told David, feeling miserable.

Paying David would cost me about a day's worth of tips. I should have just taken that lifeguard job, I thought. I'm terrible at this.

David shrugged. "I just need you to be more careful. I can't afford this sort of thing."

I nodded. So much for impressing my boss.

"The customer's always right," David continued. "I mean, that's the whole idea."

I nodded again. It was hard to imagine a person as rude as Mashed Potato Pants as being always right. I started walking away; I still had to wrap the silverware in paper napkins and refill the ketchup bottles. I just wanted to finish and get out of there.

"Hey, Caroline," David said.

I turned back around.

"If I were you, I would have dumped mashed potatoes on that guy on purpose."

I did a double take. "Really?"

He grinned. "Yeah. I'm not mad at you. In fact, when I look back on working here at the Crooked Tree Café, I think one of my favorite memories will be of Mr. Stevens standing there covered in potatoes."

I couldn't help but smile.

"Look, Caroline, you're a great server," David went on. "People tell me all the time how friendly you are. Don't worry about guys like that. You'll encounter grumpy people everywhere you work. And, yeah, you'll mess up sometimes. But the thing is, you can't let it get to you."

That made sense. "Thanks, David," I said. I felt good. In fact, I couldn't wait for my next shift.

I just hoped that no one ordered the mashed potatoes.

1. **The setting at the beginning of the passage is <u>most likely</u> intended to show that David**

   A. dislikes working at the Crooked Tree Café.

   B. enjoys keeping a certain routine after each day's rush.

   C. doesn't mind paying for Mr. Stevens's dry cleaning.

   D. is not a very effective manager of his staff.

2. **Read this sentence from the passage.**

   "His face turned as red as a stop sign, and he shouted for the manager."

   What does the writer <u>most likely</u> mean?

   A. Mr. Stevens is very angry.

   B. Mr. Stevens is serious.

   C. Mr. Stevens is sunburned.

   D. Mr. Stevens is laughing.

3. **What is the point of view of this passage?**

   A. first-person

   B. second-person

   C. third-person omniscient

   D. third-person limited

4. What will <u>most likely</u> happen next in the story? Use details from the passage and your own conclusions to support your answer.

_____

_____

_____

_____

_____

5. Explain the theme of this passage. Use details from the passage and your own conclusions to support your answer.

_____

_____

_____

_____

_____

Lesson 6: Poetry

Almost all of the literary devices we've looked at so far can apply to any type of writing, including poetry. But poems also have qualities that separate them from other kinds of literature. In the rest of this lesson, you will learn how to recognize the elements that are unique to poems.

Read the following poem. Notice the ways in which it is different from a story.

Runaway Train
by Kerry Garlett

My name is Harriet Tubman,
and I'm a train conductor.
My train makes lots of connections,
but the only destination
I know of is freedom.

My train is a runaway train,
Its passengers once slaves;
My train is a runaway train,
Never gonna be stopped.
Yes, my train is a runaway train,
but I never run my train off the track,
and I never lost a passenger.

My train is invisible;
That's why they call it "underground."
My train doesn't run on coal,
It runs on the kindness of strangers.
You don't need a ticket to get on board,
But don't forget your password.

 TIP 1: Notice the structure of the poem.

Fiction and nonfiction are divided into paragraphs. Poems are usually divided into lines and stanzas. **Lines** are rows of words. **Stanzas** are groups of lines, the "paragraphs" of the poem. Writers sometimes break lines and stanzas in unusual places to get your attention or to create a certain effect.

1. Reread the poem "Runaway Train." Why do you think the poet divides the poem into stanzas in the way that she does?

_____

_____

_____

_____

 TIP 2: Identify figurative language in poems.

As you know, figurative language is the use of words in a way that is not meant to be taken literally. If you said, "It's raining cats and dogs out there!" you would mean that it's raining very hard, not that house pets are falling from the sky. You would be speaking figuratively.

Writers often aim for fresh, original, even unusual comparisons using figures of speech. You learned about metaphors and similes in Lesson 4. Here are some other common types of figurative language.

Literal vs. Figurative

Literal meaning refers to the exact or primary meaning of words.

Figurative meaning represents an idea beyond the exact meaning of the words. It is often used to compare ideas.

Personification gives human qualities to a nonhuman thing.

> Jess knew she couldn't put off her homework much longer. Her algebra book seemed to stare at her, whisper to her, call out her name.

Imagery is a description that strongly appeals to the five senses: sight, smell, sound, taste, and touch. Writers use imagery to help readers feel like they are experiencing what the narrator or character is experiencing.

> The sweet aroma of freshly baked cookies wafted through the room as Eddie delicately removed the tray from the scorching oven, his arm soaking up the heat of the oven's rays on the otherwise frigid day.

An **analogy** is another term for a comparison. A writer may use an analogy to compare a new situation to a situation you are already familiar with.

> Giving more power to politicians is like giving your dog both ends of the leash.

CCSs: RL.8.4, L.8.5a, L.8.5b

Read the following poem. Then answer Number 2.

The Sea Wind
by Sara Teasdale

I am a pool in a peaceful place,
I greet the great sky face to face,
I know the stars and the stately moon
And the wind that runs with rippling shoon—
But why does it always bring to me
The far-off, beautiful sound of the sea?

The marsh-grass weaves me a wall of green,
But the wind comes whispering in between,
In the dead of night when the sky is deep
The wind comes waking me out of sleep—
Why does it always bring to me
The far-off, terrible call of the sea?

2. The author uses several examples of personification in the second stanza. Identify one of these examples and explain what the author means.

_____

_____

_____

_____

TIP 3: Recognize how writers play with sound.

Poetry is often written to be read aloud, so poets may use certain sound devices to make their works especially pleasing to the reader's ear. The chart below includes some common sound devices.

Sound Device	Definition	Example
alliteration	the repetition of initial consonant sounds in two or more words or syllables	Klein could be clever or clueless, kind or cold, curmudgeonly or compassionate.
assonance	the repetition of vowel sounds within words or syllables	Carrie knew that playing her favorite tune would soon lighten her mood.
consonance	the repetition of two or more consonants with different vowel sounds in between	Bill could play ball for the Bulls, but his passion was for bowling.
onomatopoeia	the use of words that sound like what they mean	Halima smacked her gum as she watched her little brother splash around in his baby pool.

Read the following poem. Then answer Number 3.

Night at the Lake

by Susan McCarty

The water is dark this late at night.
It is black silk, breeze-smoothed,
an unbroken surface, still under the moon.
The night is so quiet, I can hear my own breath,
5   The soft hitch of my lungs,
The low buzz in my ears of nothing.
I hold my breath, and it seems the night does, too.
The moon, a wide eye in the sky,
watches, unblinking.
10   Even the bullfrogs have hopped off their pulpits.
It is late and their tongues are stilled in sleep.

3. Which line from "Night at the Lake" contains the best example of assonance?

   A. line 7

   B. line 9

   C. line 10

   D. line 11

CCS: RL.8.4

 TIP 4: Listen for the "music" in the poem.

As you learned in Tip 3, most writers pay attention to how their words will sound to the reader. But this "music" plays a much bigger role in poetry than in any other kind of writing. One thing many people notice first about a poem is whether the lines rhyme. **Rhyme** is one way in which the writer creates the "music" of a poem. Not all poems have lines that rhyme, but many do.

A poem's **rhyme scheme** is the pattern of rhyming in a poem. The way to define the rhyme scheme is to mark each rhyme that comes at the end of a line with a letter of the alphabet, starting with *a*. Unmatched lines (lines that don't end in rhymes) get a letter, too. Let's use the following limerick as an example.

A mouse in her room woke Miss Doud,	*a*
Who was frightened and screamed very loud.	*a*
Then a happy thought hit her:	*b*
To scare off the critter,	*b*
She just sat up in bed and meowed.	*a*

—Writer unknown

The rhyme scheme in this poem is *aabba*. Now you try. Read this poem.

Fly away, fly away over the sea
by Christina G. Rossetti

Fly away, fly away over the sea,
Sun-loving swallow, for summer is done;
Come again, come again, come back to me,
Bringing the summer and bringing the sun.

4. What is the rhyme scheme of the poem above? _____

 TIP 5: Figure out the "beat" of the poem.

Writers add to the musicality of their poems by using rhythm. **Rhythm** is the poem's beat and is created from stressed and unstressed syllables in words. Unlike a song, in which the beat controls how and when the words are sung, a poem uses words to control the beat. By carefully choosing words based on their syllables, a writer can create a rhythmic pattern, or beat.

5. Reread the poem "Fly away, fly away over the sea." How is the rhythm of the poem like the movement of a bird?

_____

_____

TIP 6: Remember that not all poems follow the rules.

Although many poems use these rules, others do not. **Free verse** is poetry that is written without predictable rhyme or rhythm. A poem written in free verse may include rhyming words, but they are not regular.

Read the following poem. Then answer Number 6.

I Hear America Singing

by Walt Whitman

I hear America singing, the varied carols I hear,
Those of mechanics—each one singing his, as it should be, blithe and strong,
The carpenter singing his, as he measures his plank or beam,
The mason singing his, as he makes ready for work, or leaves off work,
The boatman singing what belongs to him in his boat, the deckhand singing
    on the steamboat deck,
The shoemaker singing as he sits on his bench, the hatter singing as he stands;
The wood-cutter's song, the ploughboy's, on his way in the morning, or at the
    noon intermission, or at sundown;
The delicious singing of the mother—or of the young wife at work—or of the
    girl sewing or washing, each singing what belongs to her, and to none else;
The day what belongs to the day—at night, the party of young fellows, robust,
    friendly,
Singing, with open mouths, their strong melodious songs.

6. What effect does the poet's use of free verse have on the poem?

_____

_____

_____

Lesson Practice begins on the following page.

Directions: This poem is about a maiden named Annabel Lee and her tragic fate. Read the poem. Then answer Numbers 1 through 5.

Annabel Lee

by Edgar Allan Poe

It was many and many a year ago,
In a kingdom by the sea,
That a maiden there lived whom you may know
By the name of Annabel Lee;—
5   And this maiden she lived with no other thought
Than to love and be loved by me.

She was a child and I was a child,
In this kingdom by the sea,
But we loved with a love that was more than love—
10   I and my Annabel Lee—
With a love that the winged seraphs of Heaven
Coveted her and me.

And this was the reason that, long ago,
In this kingdom by the sea,
15   A wind blew out of a cloud, by night
Chilling my Annabel Lee;
So that her highborn kinsmen came
And bore her away from me,
To shut her up in a sepulchre
20   In this kingdom by the sea.

The angels, not half so happy in Heaven,
Went envying her and me:
Yes! that was the reason (as all men know,
In this kingdom by the sea)
25   That the wind came out of the cloud, chilling
And killing my Annabel Lee.

But our love it was stronger by far than the love
Of those who were older than we—
Of many far wiser than we—
30   And neither the angels in Heaven above
Nor the demons down under the sea,
Can ever dissever my soul from the soul
Of the beautiful Annabel Lee:—

For the moon never beams without bringing me dreams
35   Of the beautiful Annabel Lee;
And the stars never rise but I see the bright eyes
Of the beautiful Annabel Lee;
And so, all the night-tide, I lie down by the side
Of my darling, my darling, my life and my bride,
40   In her sepulchre there by the sea—
In her tomb by the sounding sea.

1. **Which literary device is used in lines of the poem?**

   A.   personification

   B.   alliteration

   C.   rhyme

   D.   metaphor

2. **Line 21 contains an example of**

   A.   simile.

   B.   metaphor.

   C.   alliteration.

   D.   analogy.

3.   Which of the following words <u>best</u> describes the speaker in this poem?

   A.   worried

   B.   defeated

   C.   passive

   D.   loyal

4.   **Read these lines from the poem.**

   "And the stars never rise, but I see the bright eyes
   Of the beautiful Annabel Lee"

   What do these lines mean in the context of the poem?

   _____

   _____

   _____

   _____

5.   **How does the author use imagery to set the mood of the poem? Use details from the poem to support your answer.**

   _____

   _____

   _____

   _____

CCSs: RH.6-8.2, RST.6-8.2

Lesson 7: Literacy in History/Social Studies, Science, and Technical Subjects

In school, we often think about the subjects we study as separate areas of learning. However, being a skilled reader is the key to learning in any subject area. The important comprehension skills you learned in previous lessons can be applied to specific subject areas, such as science and history. Just like an essay or a story, a passage on the history of our political parties will have a main idea and supporting details. When you read an article on the science of climate change, you should ask yourself about the writer's point of view, just as you would when you read a persuasive essay. Strong reading skills can cross the barriers between subjects.

 TIP 1: Identify the main idea.

When you finish reading something, you should be able to tell someone what it's about in just a few sentences. This short and simple version, called the **summary**, focuses on the main idea of the work. The **main idea** is the most important idea that an author wants you to know.

Some authors state the main idea. Other authors suggest the main idea through the details they present. One way to find the main idea is to underline any important details that suggest a larger idea. Another way is to summarize what you have read as if you were explaining to someone what a text was about.

Think about main idea as you read this passage about the American Revolution.

> Many Massachusetts colonists didn't believe that the British Parliament would hear their protests. They began organizing into groups called minutemen. The name came from their promise to be ready to fight within a minute's notice. General Thomas Gage, commander of the British troops in America and military governor of Massachusetts, was not going to let a rebellion start while he was in charge. He wanted the rebel leaders arrested. Therefore, he planned to send British soldiers to Lexington, near Boston, to round them up.
>
> On the night of April 18, 1775, some colonists found out what Gage was planning. Three of them—Paul Revere, William Dawes, and Samuel Prescott—rode through the countryside to warn the minutemen that the British were coming. When British soldiers arrived, the officer leading them ordered the minutemen to go home. The minutemen, however, refused to move.

No historian is sure which side fired first, but eighteen minutemen were killed or wounded. The British marched a few miles to Concord, where they fought more minutemen. As the British marched back to Boston, angry colonists fired on them all along the way. By the end of the day, 273 British soldiers had been killed or wounded. Ninety-three Patriots had met the same fate.

1. Summarize the passage on the lines below. Be sure to include the main idea in your summary.

    _____

    _____

    _____

    _____

 TIP 2: Support ideas with details from the text.

Authors use details to make their writing more interesting and to support their main idea. **Details** are pieces of information and ideas that help writers get their message across. Details have many purposes: they can entertain us, help to explain something, or create a specific tone and mood.

Details are the building blocks of writing. Some details are more important than others. The most important details are the ones that support or explain the main idea and theme. When you're reading, ask yourself, "Is this detail important for me to understand the main idea, story, or work?" In other words, would the text still make sense even if the detail were deleted?

Read the following passage, then answer Number 2 on the next page.

Your brain is more powerful than a supercomputer. There are 100 billion microscopic cells called neurons that are constantly relaying information inside of your head. In fact, it would take more than 3,000 years to count all the neurons in your brain! Every time you read, laugh, think, talk, run, or move, chemical and electrical signals race around on neuron highways inside of you, transmitting messages to and from your brain. Your neurons send more messages than all the phones in the world. Even as you think about this, your neurons are firing! Isn't the brain an incredible part of the human body?

2. The main idea of this passage is that the brain is very powerful. Which idea is least important to the passage?

   A. . . . it would take more than 3,000 years to count all the neurons in your brain!

   B. . . . signals race around on neuron highways inside of you . . .

   C. . . . Your neurons send more messages than all the phones in the world.

   D. Isn't the brain an incredible part of the human body?

 TIP 3: **Understand how texts are organized.**

Think about newspapers, directions, and even cartoons: each of these texts tells you something in a very different way. The arrangement of ideas and information in a text is known as **text organization**. Science and social studies texts are commonly organized using one of the methods in the chart below.

Text Organization Method	Description	Example
cause and effect	The text emphasizes how actions or events cause others to take place.	a book that outlines the events that led to the start of World War I
compare and contrast	The text focuses on the similarities and differences between two people, things, or ideas.	an article that explains that gorillas and humans have similar genes, but different capabilities
sequence of events	The text portrays events in the order they occur.	steps of a science experiment that are listed in the order they should be performed to get a satisfactory result
main idea and details	The text presents a main idea, followed by the details that support it.	an essay that proposes George Washington was the most effective U.S. president, using details about his influence on the nation
question and answer	The text poses questions, followed by their answers.	a Web site that lists questions people have about the flu, followed by answers from doctors

Read the passage on the next page about how a bill becomes a law. Then answer Number 3.

CCSs: RH.6-8.3, RH.6-8.5, RH.6-8.6, RST.6-8.5, RST.6-8.6

In the U.S. Congress members of the legislature introduce bills. Presidents can also create bills for a member of the legislature to introduce. Sometimes, groups or individuals may want a bill to be considered by the legislature. Those groups or individuals can write bills, but it is still up to a member of the legislature to introduce them.

After a bill is introduced, either a House or a Senate committee studies it. The committee researches all aspects of the bill and decides whether to send it on to the full House or Senate. Although many bills are introduced in each session of Congress, only a fraction ever becomes law.

If a committee sends the bill on to the full Senate or House, the bill is debated on the floor and voted upon. Once the House or Senate has approved a bill, it is sent to the other chamber, where it goes through the same process. When the whole Congress has approved a bill, it is sent to the president. The Constitution is very specific about what happens next. The president may sign the bill into law or veto it. A vetoed bill returns to Congress. Congress may override the veto by a two-thirds majority vote in both houses.

3. Which method of text organization did the author use?

    A. question and answer

    B. compare and contrast

    C. sequence of events

    D. main idea and details

 TIP 4: Identify the author's point of view and purpose.

We all have a **point of view**. It is how we feel or think about a subject. Our point of view is not always based on facts, and others might not agree with us. An author's point of view affects the way that he or she will present information. An author can use point of view to lead the reader to believe something or feel something because of what he or she chooses to share with the reader. Other times, an author may exclude his or her point of view in order to present just the facts, or to tell things from another perspective.

There are many reasons why an author writes. An **author's purpose**, or reason, for writing might be to entertain the reader, to teach something, to reflect on an experience, or to ask readers for help.

Let's practice identifying the author's purpose and point of view. Read the following paragraph. Then answer Numbers 4 and 5.

> During the 1930s, struggling farmers of the Great Plains began grazing animals on land that had previously been used to grow crops. The grazing loosened the topsoil. Next, drought (dry weather) struck the region, including Texas. High winds stripped away the dry, loose soil, creating massive dust storms. The storms led to horrific property damage and destruction over a large area of the Great Plains, which was nicknamed the "Dust Bowl." Many innocent farmers, miners, and oil workers were forced to leave their Texas homes to find work elsewhere.

4. The author's purpose for writing this passage is

   A. to entertain the reader.

   B. to express his or her opinion.

   C. to inform the reader.

   D. to call the reader to action.

5. The author's point of view reveals that the writer thinks

   A. the Dust Bowl was a tragic event.

   B. that there were many other causes to the Dust Bowl.

   C. grazing cattle are to blame for the Dust Bowl.

   D. the people who fled the Dust Bowl were foolish.

 TIP 5: Know the differences among facts, opinions, and reasoned judgments.

Every day, we get our information from a variety of sources—friends, family, Web sites, newspapers, TV, books, and so on. It's important to know what kind of information we're getting, though. Some statements are based on truth, while others reflect personal feelings. As you read subject area texts, you will come across facts, opinions, and reasoned judgments. Review their differences in the chart on the next page.

Type of Statement	Definition	Example
fact	a piece of information that can be verified	The Jamestown Settlement was founded in 1607 in Virginia.
opinion	a personal belief or judgment that cannot be proved	Jamestown is the best place to learn about colonial America.
reasoned judgment	a statement of opinion that is supported by facts	The settlers worked long days to survive in their new land.

· Read the following passage about the Jamestown Settlement. Then answer the questions.

The Jamestown settlement was founded in 1607 on the banks of the Jamestown River in Virginia. The original colony was made up of 104 men and boys. Life in the colony was very hard. The climate was unfamiliar to the settlers, and clean water and food were scarce. Many of the settlers were members of the English upper class; consequently, the colony did not have skilled laborers and farmers.

The Jamestown settlement was located near 14,000 Algonquian Native Americans and the settlers began trading with the Native Americans for food. The first two women arrived at Jamestown the following year, in 1608. More women eventually came, but men outnumbered women for most of the 17th century. Captain John Smith became the colony's leader in September 1608 and established a "no work, no food" policy.

6. Which of the following is a fact?

   A. Women liked living in Jamestown.

   B. Captain John Smith was a cruel leader.

   C. Colonists trusted their Native American neighbors.

   D. The first women arrived at Jamestown in 1608.

7. Which of the following is a reasoned judgment about the Jamestown settlement?

   A. The colony was made up of 104 men and boys.

   B. Life in the colony was very hard.

   C. The climate was unfamiliar to the settlers.

   D. The colony did not have skilled laborers and farmers.

TIP 6: Use primary and secondary sources.

In order to find out something, such as to research the past or locate a scientific fact, you must know how to work with sources. **Sources** are materials such as encyclopedias, Web sites, journals, photos, or letters that provide information about a subject.

Sources of historical information are classified as either primary or secondary. A **primary source** is direct. If you read letters written by John Adams to his wife, Abigail, during the Revolutionary War, you are reading a primary source. As a rule, a primary source directly records the events it is connected to. Not all primary sources are written. A photo taken of Abraham Lincoln delivering the Gettysburg Address is also an example of a primary source.

A **secondary source** is indirect. If you read a book about the Revolutionary War based on the letters of John and Abigail Adams, but do not read the letters themselves, you are reading a secondary source. A secondary source is written by an author who was not directly involved in the events he or she describes.

Both sources are useful. Primary sources are the "raw materials" of social studies. Secondary sources give you another author's interpretation of the primary sources.

Watch carefully for validity and reliability of both types of sources, however. Primary sources may be inaccurate. People don't always see an event clearly when they are in the middle of everything. Like any interpretation, secondary sources are sometimes biased.

8. You want to know what life was like in the area now known as Texas during the 1500s. Which of the following might be a primary source for this information?

    A. *Early Explorers of Texas* by Winston Lujack, copyright 1987

    B. a letter from a soldier at the Alamo to his wife, written in 1836

    C. *Cabeza de Vaca's Adventures in the Unknown Interior of America* by Alvar Nuñez Cabeza de Vaca, written in about 1540

    D. a magazine article on the settlement of Galveston, copyright date unknown

9. Explain why your answer to Number 8 is correct.

    _____

    _____

    _____

TIP 7: Recognize how visual features enhance the text.

There are many ways to get information beyond just words. Charts, diagrams, graphs, or tables help to show information and add interest, design, and color to a text. Photos invite the reader to "see" a subject. These are all known as **visual features**. Done well, visual features can enhance the text and add to your understanding of the topic.

Read the passage and study the chart below. Then answer the questions.

> Immigration to the United States reached its peak between the years of 1880 and 1930. More than 24 million people entered the United States. Almost 20 million of those people entered through Ellis Island, the gateway to New York. Ellis Island opened as an immigration center in 1892. At this time, a change was happening in immigration. The number of people coming from Northern and Western European countries began to slow down, while greater numbers of immigrants from Southern and Eastern Europe began to come to America.

Immigrants to the U.S. from 1880 to 1930 (in millions)			
Italy	4.6	Britain	2.3
Austro-Hungarian Empire	4.0	Canada	2.3
Russian Empire	3.3	Ireland	1.7
German Empire	2.8	Sweden	1.1

10. According to the chart, 2.8 million immigrants came to the United States from

   A. the Russian Empire.

   B. the German Empire.

   C. Britain.

   D. Canada.

11. Which information included in the chart is not included in the article?

   A. the number of immigrants who came to the U.S. from 1880 to 1930

   B. the number of people who came through Ellis Island

   C. the changes to immigration laws during the early 1900s

   D. the names of the countries most immigrants came from

TIP 8: Follow directions.

Directions give step-by-step information on how to do something. Before beginning a task, it's important to read all directions, or instructions, from beginning to end. Directions frequently present information in a numbered or bulleted list.

The order of the list is important. You must complete every step of the process in order to successfully accomplish the task. For example, if you wanted to accurately measure the distance you walk each day between your home and your school, you would have to walk your exact route using a pedometer to count your steps. If you went a different way, forgot to turn on the pedometer, or turned back too early, you would not get the correct distance.

Read the following directions, then answer Numbers 12 and 13.

How to Make Hard-Boiled Eggs

1. Place five eggs in a large pot. The pot should be large enough so that the eggs don't bump into each other.
2. Cover the eggs with one inch of cold water. The water should be just over the tops of the eggs.
3. Add one teaspoon of salt to the water to increase the water temperature.
4. Cover the pot with a tight-fitting lid and set on the stove.
5. Turn the burner on the high setting.
6. Bring the water to a rolling boil (about six minutes).
7. Turn off the burner and, using pot holders, move the pot to a cold burner.
8. Let sit for 30 minutes until fully cooled.

12. According to the directions, which of the following steps should be completed first?

    A. Cover the eggs with one inch of cold water.

    B. Turn the burner on the high setting.

    C. Add one teaspoon of salt to the water.

    D. Bring the water to a rolling boil.

13. Based on the information above, you can infer that you should

    A. fill the pot to the top with warm water before boiling.

    B. use a lid slightly larger than the pot as the eggs are boiling.

    C. set a timer for 30 minutes to make sure the eggs are cooked.

    D. choose a pot where the eggs can touch each other as they are cooking.

TIP 9: Determine the meanings of content-related words and phrases.

When you come across an unfamiliar word as you read, you can sometimes figure out the meaning of the word by looking at the words around it. This is called using context. **Context** refers to the words and sentences around a word that help you to figure out the word's meaning. For example, read the following sentence.

> On the windiest day of the year, the <u>anemometer</u> measured gusts at 44 miles per hour.

In this sentence, you can figure out that the word *anemometer* must mean an instrument to measure wind speed. The words *windiest*, *gusts*, and *44 miles per hour* are clues that point to the meaning of *anemometer*.

Sometimes you can figure out the meaning of an unfamiliar word because the author restates the meaning in another way. Other times, you might find a clue that hints at the word's opposite meaning. When reading scientific or technical material, sometimes an author will define the word right in the text, or put a footnote next to the word.

14. Read this sentence.

    The supplies were *depleted*. Medicine was scarce, and there was not enough food and water left to sustain the soldiers.

    Which of the following is the best definition of *depleted*?

    A. restored

    B. used up

    C. wasted

    D. delivered

 TIP 10: Compare and contrast information from multiple sources.

As you have learned, when you compare and contrast, you decide in what ways things are alike and different. For example, if you were to compare and contrast how you live today with how the Pilgrims lived when they settled in Massachusetts, you would see many differences—like the fact that they dressed strangely and didn't have the modern conveniences of electricity or machines. Yet you might also see many similarities, such as parents raising children, people working together in a community, and a society that values hard work. Comparing and contrasting is a very useful tool in science and social studies texts, since it can help the reader understand a new concept in terms of something they already know.

Read the passages on the next page, then respond to Number 15.

What Are Comets?

Comets are small chunks of dust and rock held together by ice. Each comet is a little different, but astronomers think that 80% of the ice is frozen water, 15% of it is carbon monoxide, and the rest is a combination of other chemicals. Each comet has its own unique orbit.

The solid part of a comet, the nucleus, is just a few kilometers across. Because the nucleus is small, comets are invisible from Earth—until they approach the Sun. Then, some of the ice turns to gas and forms a glowing head called a coma. The coma can be as large as 100,000 km across. Streams of particles from the Sun, called the solar wind, push the gases away from the comet. Photons of light also press against escaping dust particles, creating a second tail. These tails can stretch as far as 100 million kilometers. When we observe a comet from Earth, we are seeing its coma and tails.

Caroline Herschel: Astronomer

As a young girl in Germany, Caroline Herschel was very bright and loved music. At age 23, she went to live with her older brother William, who was a professor of music in England. There, she was a professional singer and studied mathematics and astronomy, as well. William also became something of an expert in astronomy and wanted Caroline to assist him in his research. Caroline gave up her music to help her brother. After William discovered the planet Uranus, the king asked him to be Great Britain's Royal Astronomer; the king later hired Caroline, too. She became the first woman to discover a comet (in all, she discovered eight comets), and she discovered 14 nebulae (collections of gas and dust in space). She was awarded several gold medals in science, and to this day, no one has ever found an error in her mathematical calculations.

15. Compare and contrast these passages on the lines below.

_____

_____

_____

_____

_____

Lesson Practice begins on the following page.

Directions: This is a speech delivered by President Abraham Lincoln. Read this speech. Then answer Numbers 1 through 4.

The Gettysburg Address

President Abraham Lincoln gave this speech at the dedication of the Soldiers' National Cemetery in Gettysburg, Pennsylvania, on November 19, 1863. The Civil War was still in progress.

Four score and seven years ago our fathers brought forth on this continent, a new nation, conceived in Liberty, and dedicated to the proposition[1] that all men are created equal.

Now we are engaged in a great civil war, testing whether that nation, or any nation so conceived and so dedicated, can long endure. We are met on a great battlefield of that war. We have come to dedicate a portion of that field, as a final resting place for those who here gave their lives that that nation might live. It is altogether fitting and proper that we should do this.

But, in a larger sense, we cannot dedicate—we cannot consecrate—we cannot hallow[2]—this ground. The brave men, living and dead, who struggled here, have consecrated it, far above our poor power to add or detract[3]. The world will little note, nor long remember what we say here, but it can never forget what they did here. It is for us the living, rather, to be dedicated here to the unfinished work which they who fought here have thus far so nobly advanced. It is rather for us to be here dedicated to the great task remaining before us—that from these honored dead we take increased devotion to that cause for which they gave the last full measure of devotion—that we here highly resolve that these dead shall not have died in vain—that this nation, under God, shall have a new birth of freedom— and that government of the people, by the people, for the people, shall not perish from the earth.

[1]**proposition:** topic under consideration
[2]**consecrate, hallow:** make sacred
[3]**detract:** take away from

1. **This speech by President Lincoln is considered a primary source document because**

    A. people remember these famous words.

    B. it is printed in many textbooks.

    C. many people agree with the ideas expressed by Lincoln.

    D. President Lincoln wrote and delivered the speech.

2. **Read this sentence from the passage.**

    "The brave men, living and dead, who struggled here, have consecrated it, far above our poor power to add or detract."

    Which words in this sentence help you determine the meaning of *detract*?

    A.   "our poor power"

    B.   "living and dead"

    C.   "add or"

    D.   "the brave men"

3. **Which of the following phrases from the passage** <u>best</u> **states the main idea?**

    A.   "…dedicated to the proposition that all men are created equal."

    B.   "Now we are engaged in a great civil war…"

    C.   "We have come to dedicate a portion of that field…"

    D.   "The world will little note…what we say here…"

4. **Describe President Lincoln's purpose for writing and delivering this speech.**

    _____

    _____

    _____

    _____

Directions: This passage describes how the oceans provide water to the water cycle through evaporation. The experiment that follows demonstrates how evaporation takes place. Read this passage and experiment. Then answer Numbers 5 through 9.

The Ocean and the Water Cycle—Nature's Storehouse

Although about 70 percent of Earth's surface is water, most of the water is found in the world's oceans. In fact, 96 percent of the water on this planet is in the oceans. So we're surrounded by water, but much of it is loaded with saline, which is dissolved salt. Scientists have discovered a way to remove the saline from water through a process called desalination, but it is very expensive to do. However, nature has another use for the water in the oceans. The water in the ocean is part of a great storehouse. This is because when water evaporates from the ocean into the atmosphere, it leaves behind its saline and enters the water cycle. It's estimated that the oceans supply about 90 percent of the evaporated water that goes into the water cycle.

Imagine a drop of water on the surface of the sea. The sun warms it, and it evaporates in water vapor, leaving its saline behind in the ocean. The vapor then rises as strong winds carry it over the land. The vapor changes back to a liquid through a process called condensation and combines with particles of dust, smoke, and salt crystals to become part of a cloud.

When this drop of water combines with other drops, it forms a bigger drop and falls to the earth as rain. The drop could land on the ground and stay there for some time, or it might fall in a lake or even back in the ocean, where evaporation could take place all over again. So the next time you look at a cloud, you might be looking at drops of ocean water that have evaporated into the sky!

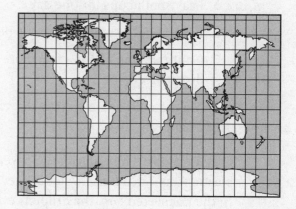

Evaporation Experiment

Materials Needed

- 2 large clear plastic cups
- Pen or marker
- Clear plastic wrap
- Rubber band
- Water
- Salt

Directions

1. Fill the plastic cups with water so that they both have 6 ounces of water.

2. Add one teaspoon of salt to both cups.

3. Mark the levels of the water with the pen on the outside of the cup.

4. Cover one of the cups with plastic wrap and wrap the rubber band around the rim to keep the plastic wrap tightly in place.

5. Leave both cups for one day.

6. Look at both cups and use the pen to mark if the water level has gone down.

7. Continue step #5 for a few more days, until the water in the uncovered cup has disappeared.

8. Make a note on how many days it took for the water in the uncovered cup to disappear.

Observations: The water in the covered cup will not go down. This is because the plastic wrap catches the water as it evaporates, and the droplets fall back into the cup. In the uncovered cup, the droplets evaporate into the air, leaving behind only the salt.

5. **The map reinforces the main idea of the passage by showing that**

    A. the northern part of the world has the most land.

    B. the world is mostly water.

    C. there are many continents.

    D. Asia is the biggest continent.

6. **Which information is included in <u>both</u> the passage and the experiment?**

    A. When salt water evaporates in the air, it leaves behind the salt.

    B. Water stays in the same general place, even after it evaporates.

    C. Vapor that rises from the ocean always ends up back in the ocean.

    D. The water in the covered cup slowly loses its salt.

7. **In the experiment, which step should you complete <u>first</u>?**

    A. Add salt to each cup.

    B. Cover one cup with plastic wrap.

    C. Fill both cups with the same amount of water.

    D. Mark if the level of water has gone down.

8. What are some ways that you can verify, or prove, that the information in "The Ocean and the Water Cycle—Nature's Storehouse" is factual?

_____

_____

_____

_____

9. Which method of text organization does the author use in "Evaporation Experiment"? Explain whether or not this method is effective.

_____

_____

_____

_____

UNIT 2

Writing

Now that you know how to identify and interpret various kinds of reading, it's time to focus on the flip side: writing. To be a writer, the most important thing is to have an idea. An idea gives you a reason to write. The next thing you need is a way to organize your idea so that it will make sense to others. And last, you need to be able to use language to make your ideas compelling.

In this unit, you'll learn how to plan, draft, and revise your writing. Whether you're writing a story about a young girl's first dance, composing a letter to the principal of your school about the shortage of bike racks, or writing your own life story, the tips in this unit will help turn you into a great writer.

In This Unit

CCSs: W.8.4, WHST.6-8.4

Lesson 8: Writing for a Purpose

Imagine you are a student in Mr. Brown's English class. Mr. Brown assigns your class so much reading that no one has time to do anything else. (Thirty-eight books a week is just too much!) Your class wants to write a letter to Mr. Brown explaining why they would like to have fewer reading assignments. If you were given this writing task, what would you do first?

TIP 1: Know what type of writing you are doing.

Before you can start putting your thoughts down on paper, you have to identify the basic type of writing you plan to do. Here are some common types of writing.

narrative	This type of writing involves describing an event or series of events that are true or made up. Creative stories, expressive personal essays, poetry, and drama are all kinds of narrative writing.
argument	This type of writing, sometimes called persuasive writing, is used to influence readers to agree with the author's opinion. Sometimes the author wants readers to take a particular action. Letters to the editor, advertisements, and problem-solution essays are a few kinds of arguments.
informational	This type of writing provides facts about a real-world topic or task. Examples of informational writing include reports, invitations, directions, manuals, formal letters, memos, recipes, and schedules.
literary response	This type of writing involves reading a text carefully, interpreting it, and describing how the writer uses certain devices to affect his or her audience. Book reports and essays based on texts are examples of literary response.

1. What basic type of writing will you be doing when you write your letter to Mr. Brown?

_____

CCSs: W.8.4, WHST.6-8.4

 TIP 2: Understand your purpose and know your audience.

It is important to know why you are writing and who you are writing for. This helps you decide what ideas and details should be a part of your work.

To help you understand the purpose and audience of your writing, answer the following questions every time you write:

- **What is the writing topic?** The topic is what the writing is about.
- **Who is the audience?** The audience is who will read the work.
- **What is the purpose?** The purpose is the main reason for writing.
- **What form will the writing take?** The form is the kind of writing, such as an essay, a story, a letter, or a journal entry.

For the letter to Mr. Brown, the answers would look like this:

- What is the writing topic?

  the amount of reading homework given by the teacher

- Who is the audience?

  the teacher, Mr. Brown

- What is the purpose?

  to persuade Mr. Brown that assigning less reading is a good idea

- What form will the writing take?

  a letter

Reporters' Questions

All reporters carry along at least six tools with them wherever they go. These are the questions *Who? What? When? Where? Why?* and *How?*

Use these questions to help you understand any topic and gather ideas for writing about this topic.

TIP 3: Your purpose and audience affect every part of your writing.

The purpose and audience of your writing are central to any writing assignment. They affect everything from the content and basic form of what you write to the kinds of words you use (formal, slang, or somewhere in between). For example, if you want to entertain your readers, you might write a story. If, however, you want to inform your readers, you might instead choose to write an article or a report.

Here are some common purposes for writing:

- to entertain with a made-up story
- to inform readers about a specific topic
- to communicate an idea
- to persuade readers to share a certain opinion
- to describe something, such as an event or a place
- to explain how to do something

TIP 4: Know your audience.

You speak differently to your friends than you do to your teacher, right? These are different audiences. The same thing applies to writing. Imagine that you've decided to run for student body president. As part of your campaign, you need to write a letter to a faculty advisor outlining your platform—the changes you'd like to make, your plans for the school year, etc. You also have to write a letter to your classmates, outlining the same things. Your tone in the letter to the faculty advisor should be professional and respectful, so she takes you and your ideas seriously. In comparison, the letter to your peers can be more lighthearted. You still want to persuade them to vote for you, but they need to identify with you and will probably appreciate a more relaxed tone.

Since your audience will affect everything you write, from the words you use to the context you give, it's often helpful to picture an actual person from the audience you are writing for. When writing for a test, try to imagine a person who has very high standards such as your teacher or a test scorer. Try to anticipate how this person would respond to your ideas and word choices.

CCSs: W.8.4, WHST.6-8.4

Writing for an adult audience needs to contain mostly formal language. This is especially true if the piece of writing is formal itself, such as a response to literature or a research report. Casual language and slang can be effective in some types of writing, such as short stories. The important thing is to know when to use casual language and slang and when not to.

Imagine the following scenarios. Try to imagine how you would write for each audience.

2. You are writing a report on *The Adventures of Tom Sawyer* for English class. Who is your audience? What should your tone and language choice convey?

_____

_____

_____

3. You are writing a story about a young kid who discovers a secret room in his house. Who is your audience? What type of language or tone would you use?

_____

_____

_____

 TIP 5: Responses to literature are more than summarizing.

Literature often presents us with multiple meanings, so analyzing it can be both challenging and rewarding. When you analyze literature, you attempt to understand the full meaning of it.

You can craft responses to both fiction and nonfiction texts, but there are certain rules that apply no matter what genre you are discussing. You should be able to describe how the writer uses certain devices to affect his or her audience. You should be able to connect your own responses to the writer's use of literary devices and to specific parts of the text. You should also be able to back up your judgments with references to the text and to your personal knowledge and experience. You will learn more about writing responses to literature in Lesson 15.

Lesson Practice begins on the following page.

Directions: Read the writing prompt. Then answer Numbers 1 through 4.

Imagine that your neighbors have asked you to take care of their cat while they are on vacation. After they return, you find that they have left money in your mailbox as payment, even though you told them you would be happy to take care of their cat for free. In a note to your neighbors, thank them for the money, but also explain that you enjoy taking care of their cat and do not really expect to be paid every time.

---

1. **What is the topic of the writing?**

   _____

   _____

2. **Who is the audience?**

   _____

   _____

3. **What is the purpose?**

   _____

   _____

4. **What form will the writing take?**

   _____

   _____

CCSs: W.8.5, WHST.6-8.4, WHST.6-8.5

Lesson 9: Planning

In this lesson, you will learn different prewriting strategies to help you think of and arrange ideas for your writing.

 TIP 1: When you brainstorm, you create a "storm" of ideas in your mind.

When you **brainstorm**, you write down any idea that pops into your head—no matter how strange or silly that idea might seem at the time. You want ideas to pour down like rain. Your goal is to write down as many ideas as you can as fast as lightning.

Brainstorming doesn't have to be neat. You can brainstorm your ideas in the form of a list, or you can write notes all over the page. You might want to brainstorm on a separate piece of scratch paper. Many students find it helpful to make brainstorming webs because it lets them see how their ideas are connected.

Suppose you were given the following writing prompt:

> Most people have places where they enjoy spending time. Think of a place you especially like. It might be a place you've gone on vacation or a place you go every week, such as the shopping mall or public library. Write an informational essay telling about one of your favorite places and why you like it there.

Your brainstorming web might look like this:

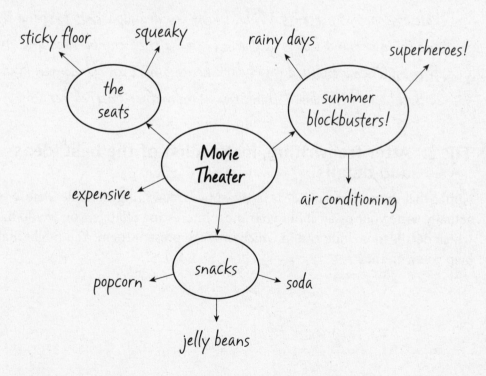

CCSs: W.8.5, WHST.6-8.4, WHST.6-8.5

 TIP 2: **Freewriting, like brainstorming, is a quick way to generate ideas.**

Another good way to come up with ideas in a hurry is to use an activity called freewriting. When you **freewrite**, you write nonstop about a topic as fast as you can.

A minute or two is usually enough time to come up with a lot of ideas. Don't worry about grammar, punctuation, capitalization, or spelling. The most important thing about freewriting is to keep writing.

Suppose you were trying to come up with ideas for an expository essay on your most interesting relative. Your freewriting might look like this:

> My grandmother Frances Thompson is my most interesting relative. She wears red lipstick all the time. Flowery dresses with tight wastes and full skirts. Manages to have a conversation with just about everyone she meets. Knows the names of all the waiters in her favorite restaurant and of the checkout people at her usual grocery store. My grandfather Theodore Thompson is a very quiet person. When I was little, I was afraid of him because he's so quiet. Silence made him seem stern. Now his quietness makes him seem sweet. Granny Franny talks all the time. Her hand gestures and her laugh are big and dramatic. She remembers details of everyone's lives. Once brought me and my sister fish-shaped sunglasses and kaleidoscopes as presents. When I visit my grandparents to spend the night, one thing she and I do is go driving around the neighborhood and visit her friends. Once we visited a sad dark house where an old woman lived alone with a hairy little dog. I think my grandmother cheered her up.

TIP 3: **After freewriting, make a list of the best ideas and details.**

Notice that there are many ideas in the above freewriting example. Before you could actually write your essay about your most interesting relative, you would have to select which details to include and in which order to present them. You might make a list to help you with this.

118

CCSs: W.8.5, WHST.6-8.4, WHST.6-8.5

 Practice Activity 1

Directions: The prompt on page 117 asked about a place where you enjoy spending time. On the following lines, freewrite about one or more of your favorite places.

_____

_____

_____

_____

_____

_____

_____

_____

_____

_____

 TIP 4: Create a clear focus.

Once you've generated several ideas for your paper, you'll need to choose one idea to write about. The **focus** of your paper is the main idea. By choosing a controlling idea, you'll be able to more thoroughly cover your topic. You'll write a much better paper if you focus on one topic instead of listing ten different topics without giving any facts or details to support those topics.

Once you have a main focus, see if you need to find out more about the idea. For example, if you are writing about your favorite relative, you might ask to interview him or her. If you are writing about a current event, on the other hand, you might read online articles or watch the news.

Make sure the information you are getting is valid and reliable. **Valid** means that the point an author is making is based on facts or logical reasoning. **Reliable** means that the information is coming from a well-respected or educated source.

TIP 5: Graphic organizers can help you get your ideas in order.

Graphic organizers help you organize your ideas to fit your focus and the type of writing you are doing. They show how ideas are connected. They can help you compare and contrast ideas, plan a story's plot, explain ideas, give opinions and supporting arguments, or show causes and effects.

Charts, tables, and graphs are three examples of graphic organizers you've seen before. You may also be familiar with **Venn diagrams**, which show similarities and differences between different groups of things. Use a Venn diagram like the one below to plan a paper in which you will compare ideas or things.

Compare/Contrast

Subject A   Subject B

Differences   Similarities   Differences

A **story map** is a type of graphic organizer that can help you plan a story or narrative essay. You will work with a story map in the Practice Activity on the next page.

CCSs: W.8.5, WHST.6-8.4, WHST.6-8.5

Practice Activity 2

Directions: Fill out the following story map about your favorite book.

Story Map

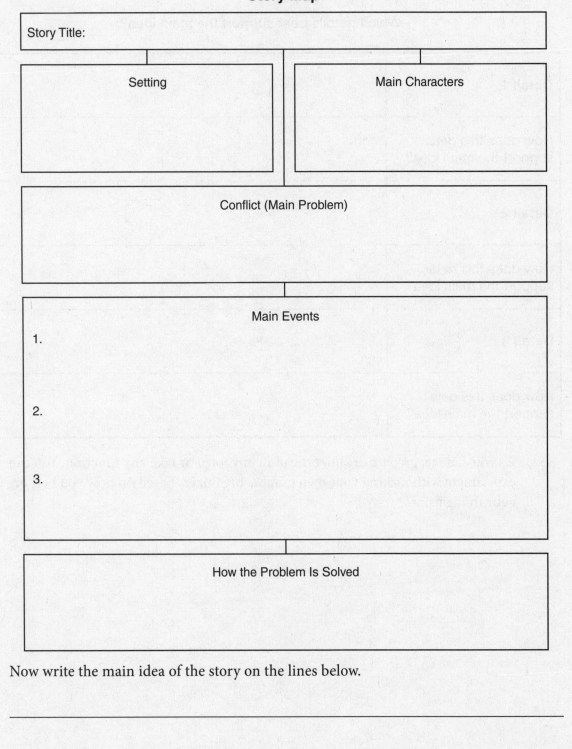

Now write the main idea of the story on the lines below.

_____

_____

CCSs: W.8.5, WHST.6-8.4, WHST.6-8.5

 ## Practice Activity 3

Directions: Use the following graphic organizer to organize the details in the story that support the main idea.

Which details best support the main idea?

Detail 1	
How does this detail support the main idea?	
Detail 2	
How does this detail support the main idea?	
Detail 3	
How does this detail support the main idea?	

As you can see, graphic organizers can fit any form or take any function. You can experiment with making your own graphic organizers based on how you best organize your thoughts.

CCSs: W.8.5, WHST.6-8.4, WHST.6-8.5

 TIP 6: **Choose the best format for your writing.**

Remember, the **format** is the type of writing you do and how you organize your information. Think about the purpose of your writing and your audience when making decisions about organization.

For example, for an informational essay that compares and contrasts the viewpoints of two politicians, you might first describe all the similarities between the viewpoints, and then discuss the differences. For a narrative about how you spent your summer, you may want to discuss events in the order that they happened.

 TIP 7: **Well-organized writing often has three main parts: an introduction, a body, and a conclusion.**

By this point, you've brainstormed, conducted a freewrite, and arranged (and rearranged) your ideas in graphic organizers. The next step is getting your ideas in an order your audience can easily follow. Most kinds of writing, especially reports and essays, have three major parts. The chart below lists these parts.

Part	Where It Is	What It Includes
introduction	the beginning	An introduction should capture the reader's attention with an engaging opening. It should clearly state the subject and let the reader know what to expect in the rest of the writing. The introduction is usually a single paragraph.
body	the middle	The body includes the writer's main points, along with details that support those main points. In a narrative, the body is the "story—the actual telling of events as they happened. The body usually consists of several paragraphs.
conclusion	the end	The conclusion finishes the writing, usually by tying up all the main points into a single closing idea. The best conclusions give the reader something to think about after they are finished reading. The conclusion is usually one paragraph long.

Practice Activity 4

Directions: Read the prompt and answer the questions that follow. On the next page, brainstorm or freewrite ideas for a response. Then, create a graphic organizer to organize your ideas.

> The high school you will attend next year is looking for movie reviewers to write for the student newspaper next fall. In order to be considered for the job, write an essay describing why you love your favorite movie. Be sure to support your ideas with details.

1. What is the topic of the writing?

   _____

2. Who is the audience?

   _____

3. What is the purpose?

   _____

4. What form will the writing take?

   _____

CCSs: W.8.5, WHST.6-8.4, WHST.6-8.5

Brainstorm or freewrite in the following space.

Create a graphic organizer to begin organizing your response.

Lesson Practice begins on the following page.

125

Planning

Make a plan for an essay about your favorite summertime activity. It may be something as simple as going to the neighborhood pool or mowing your lawn. Think about what this activity entails, how often you do it, and why you enjoy it.

Writer's Checklist

✓ **A complete essay plan:**

☐ organizes ideas for the essay.

☐ focuses on a main idea.

☐ includes important details.

☐ uses the correct format.

Directions: Brainstorm ideas for your essay in the space below.

Directions: Create a graphic organizer from the ideas you have brainstormed. Plan your essay in the space below.

CCSs: W.8.4, WHST.6-8.4

Lesson 10: Drafting

In Lesson 9, you learned that the basic structure of writing includes three parts: the introduction, the body, and the conclusion.

Typically, the introduction is a single paragraph. The body of the paper contains multiple paragraphs organized in a way that makes the most sense to the reader. The conclusion is commonly a single paragraph as well. In this lesson, you will learn how to write well-organized and easy-to-follow paragraphs.

 TIP 1: **Develop each paragraph around a single idea and its supporting details.**

A good paragraph is created with a single, clear idea. Every sentence in a paragraph should relate to the same idea. Sentences within a paragraph also need to clearly connect to one another in an order that makes sense. Additionally, each paragraph in your writing will connect back to the main focus, or topic, of the writing.

 TIP 2: **A well-organized paragraph has three parts.**

Like a well-organized paper, each paragraph has three main parts:

- The **topic sentence** tells the main idea of the paragraph. It is often, but not always, the first sentence in the paragraph.

- The **body** of the paragraph supports the main idea with details, reasons, examples, or other supporting information that connect to the topic sentence.

- The **closing sentence** ties the details of the paragraph together and helps relate the paragraph to the focus, or main idea, of the paper. The closing sentence can also give hints about what the next paragraph will say.

 TIP 3: **The topic sentence clearly states what the paragraph is about.**

The topic sentence does not need to be the first sentence in the paragraph, but it often is. A topic sentence helps the writer by serving as a reference point for the rest of the sentences in the paragraph. If your sentences don't connect to the original topic, you know that it's time for a new paragraph with a new topic sentence.

Read the following excerpt from the book "Elvis Up Close," edited by Rose Clayton and Dick Heard. The excerpt is written from the point of view of Elvis's band members.

_____ The noise was so loud we couldn't hear him play; we had to watch him. D.J., being an old drummer, could follow Elvis and take cues from his body motions and get us through it. Maybe we'd hear a faint echo once in a while bouncing back from the auditorium. It was difficult. It really was. The audience would scream and we'd get bits and pieces, but for the most part we couldn't hear him.

1. Which topic sentence best fits in the blank?

    A. Elvis played a mean guitar.

    B. Elvis's first concerts were wild confusion.

    C. Elvis's first concerts were not very popular.

    D. The ticket office usually had a long line.

Openings and Closings

The opening of your paper should grab your readers' attention and make them want to keep on reading. Here are some ideas for opening your paper:

• Tell a brief story or joke.
• Ask a question.
• Give a quotation.
• Make a dramatic or shocking statement.
• Hint at what your conclusion will be.
• Present an astonishing fact that your readers may not know.

Conclude your paper with a paragraph that wraps up your discussion of the topic. You might do one or more of the following:

• Restate your main idea, stressing its importance.
• Summarize the main points.
• Recommend an action.
• Predict an outcome.
• Give a warning.

CCSs: W.8.4, WHST.6-8.4

 TIP 4: After you decide on a topic sentence, add details to support it.

Once you state an idea in your topic sentence, it's important to add details to support that idea. Remember, your job is to help your reader understand your ideas. Write each sentence as clearly as possible, and arrange the sentences in a way that makes the most sense.

2. Read the following topic sentence.

   Louisa May Alcott is best known for writing the book *Little Women*, but she also played an important role in supporting women's rights.

   Which detail best supports this topic sentence?

   A. She was born on November 29, 1832, in Pennsylvania.

   B. At the time, it was rare for a woman to work outside of the home, but the wages she earned from the success of her books helped support her family.

   C. Madelon Bedell wrote a biography about Alcott and her family called *The Alcotts: A Family Biography*.

   D. Alcott moved to Boston, Massachusetts, at the age of 2.

Supporting Details

Good supporting details are:

- relevant, or connected, to the topic.

- specific and significant.

- appropriate for the intended audience.

Details can include any of the following:

- anecdotes

- specific examples

- reasons

- facts and statistics

- definitions

- events

- descriptions

- actions

- dialogue

CCSs: W.8.4, WHST.6-8.4

 TIP 5: Make sure every sentence in the paragraph supports the topic.

Information unrelated to your topic will make your paragraph disorganized and difficult to understand. Be sure every one of your sentences connects to and supports the topic sentence of the paragraph.

Read the following paragraph, then answer Number 3.

(1) In-line skating became popular in the '90s, but many still enjoy the sport today. (2) Elm City has an in-line skate club called "Elm City Rollers." (3) In addition to holding events in Elm City, Elm City Rollers connects other fans of in-line skating across the United States. (4) Ice skaters also use the Internet to find places to go skating.

3. Which sentence does not belong in the paragraph?

   A. sentence 1

   B. sentence 2

   C. sentence 3

   D. sentence 4

 TIP 6: A concluding sentence should wrap up a paragraph's information and lead the reader into the next paragraph.

The word *closure* means "the feeling of completeness." You should try to give each paragraph in your writing some closure. You can do that by ending each paragraph with a concluding sentence. Ideally, your concluding sentence will be more than just the last in a series of details. The sentence should be a way of wrapping up the information that comes before it. Also, it might hint at ideas to come in the next paragraph.

4. Write a sentence that completes the paragraph about in-line skating.

_____

_____

_____

CCSs: W.8.4, WHST.6-8.4

 TIP 7: **The introductory paragraph states the topic and purpose of your paper.**

The first paragraph of a paper has an important job. Not only does it need to grab your readers' attention, it also needs to tell them what you are writing and why.

The focus, or topic, of your paper is the main idea. Your focus should be clear in the introduction. Usually the topic sentence of the introductory paragraph tells the main idea of the whole paper.

Each of the following paragraphs of the paper will connect or relate back to the topic discussed in the introduction.

The purpose, or reason why you are writing your paper, is also included in the introduction. Remember the common purposes for writing:

- to inform your reader about a subject
- to persuade your reader to do something or think about a topic in a certain way
- to entertain readers with a made-up story
- to communicate an idea
- to describe something, such as an event or a place
- to explain how to do something

TIP 8: **The concluding paragraph of your paper needs to restate the topic and purpose.**

Your conclusion should wrap up all the details and ideas you included in your paper into a final thought. That final thought should also connect back to the topic and purpose stated in the introduction.

Practice Activity 1

Directions: Read the following paragraph. Then answer Numbers 1 and 2.

(1) Andrew Carnegie has one of the most well known rags-to-riches stories. (2) He emigrated from Scotland to the United States as a child and then grew up and built the Carnegie Steel Company. (3) He became a smart businessman, making decisions that later made him the second-richest man in history. (4) But Carnegie remembered his roots in poverty and donated most of his money to build schools, libraries, and universities.

1. Which sentence is the topic sentence of the paragraph?

   A. sentence 1

   B. sentence 2

   C. sentence 3

   D. sentence 4

2. Which sentence is the concluding sentence of the paragraph?

   A. sentence 1

   B. sentence 2

   C. sentence 3

   D. sentence 4

CCSs: W.8.4, WHST.6-8.4

 Practice Activity 2

Directions: Put the following paragraphs in the order that makes the most sense. Place a number in the blank next to the paragraph to indicate which paragraph should come first, second, and third.

_____ The Benjamin Franklin Bridge in Philadelphia, Pennsylvania, was completed in 1926. The bridge was designed by an architect named Paul Philippe Cret and was the largest bridge built at the time. The bridge, originally named the Delaware River Port Authority Bridge, crosses over the Delaware River and connects Philadelphia to Camden, New Jersey.

_____ The size and beauty of the bridge remind drivers and onlookers of the impact that Benjamin Franklin had on our society. Built to connect two places with a long history of creating and fulfilling American dreams, the bridge is also a reminder that no task is too small. With the right people's talents, like the creativity of Paul Philippe Cret and the strength of the many workers who built the bridge, anything is possible.

_____ In 1956, the Delaware Port Authority decided to rename the bridge to honor one of the state's greatest members, Benjamin Franklin. Franklin was a great scientist and patriot. His inventions, such as bifocal lenses, the lightning rod used to protect buildings and ships from lightning damage, and the Franklin stove that was used in homes to keep them warm, were not his only gifts. Franklin was also a writer. He penned many books over the years, some under pseudonyms, but was known best for writing *Poor Richard's Almanac* and *The Pennsylvania Gazette*.

Tying It All Together

Once you have a clear topic sentence, body, and conclusion, you can work on connecting your ideas so that they make sense to your reader. For your paper to flow smoothly, the paragraphs can't be completely separate from each other. Even though the paragraphs deal with separate ideas, they all should link together like boxcars in a train. They should smoothly take your reader from the introductory paragraph (the engine), through the body paragraphs (the boxcars), to a logical conclusion (the caboose).

Without couplers (hitches between railroad cars), a train would fall apart. In much the same way, your paper requires transitions to keep the ideas connected.

 TIP 9: Sentences need to connect in some way.

Reading what other people write can give you a window into how they think. Likewise, your own writing is a way to communicate how you think. Don't assume that your ideas are as clear to your reader as they are to you. Make sure that every sentence you write is connected to the ones before and after it.

Use the following paragraph to answer Number 5.

(1) I have never really liked cooking. (2) But Cameron convinced me to take a cooking class last month. (3) First, our teacher asked us to grab a partner and prepare a simple meal that we make often. (4) Cameron and I made macaroni and cheese. (5) We both make this so often that we can practically make it in our sleep! (6) We couldn't use a box or a prepared mix. (7) So, we got creative and looked through the pantry and the refrigerator for ingredients. (8) It turned out that the recipe that we came up with was so much better than the boxed kind. (9) Now I love cooking, and Cameron and I always make our new "Mac n' cheese" recipe for our friends.

5. Read this sentence.

   The only problem was that we had to make it from scratch.

   Where should this sentence best fit in the paragraph above?

   A. after sentence 1

   B. after sentence 5

   C. after sentence 6

   D. after sentence 8

CCSs: W.8.4, WHST.6-8.4

 TIP 10: Paragraph transitions keep your ideas moving smoothly.

Transitions are words, phrases, or sentences that help show your reader how one idea is connected to the next. They also make your writing easier to read by smoothing out the breaks between paragraphs.

For example, read the following two paragraphs from an essay about the dangers facing our national parks.

> Believe it or not, our national parks are suffering because of their popularity. Many of the most famous parks have millions of visitors each year. This means more litter, more cars, and more land converted for human use (campgrounds, picnic areas, and so on). It also means less land for the plants and animals that live there.
>
> Pollution hurts our national parks. Even when they are far from big cities, parks are affected by the chemicals used in modern society. Many scientists believe that pollutants in the air cause the thinning of the ozone layer, the part of the atmosphere that protects the earth from the sun's most harmful rays. These rays could damage many of the plant and animal species that parks are supposed to preserve. Pollution also enters national parks through the rivers that run through them, poisoning the fish and water plants, and endangering other wildlife.

First, identify the main points of each paragraph.

6. Write a one-sentence summary of the main idea in the first paragraph.

_____

_____

7. Now write a one-sentence summary of the main idea in the second paragraph.

_____

_____

Although each paragraph focuses on its own specific idea, both relate to the overall subject of the essay: the dangers facing our national parks. However, there's no connection between these paragraphs in the actual report. The author simply skips from one idea to the next. Using a transition at the end of the first paragraph or at the beginning of the second paragraph would help the reader follow the ideas more easily.

There is no perfect formula for creating a transition. If a word, phrase, or sentence logically links two paragraphs, it's a successful transition. There are, however, several specific words and phrases that are often used in transitions. Many times, just a word or two will do the job.

Transition words and phrases can help you make different kinds of connections. The following chart lists the types of connections you can make, along with example words and phrases you can use:

Function	Transition
to add more facts	to begin with, also, again, another, next, in addition
to compare	also, as, in the same way, similarly, likewise
to emphasize	but, although, despite, even though, however, instead, yet, on the other hand, otherwise
to draw a conclusion	in fact, indeed, of course, certainly
to give an example	for example, in particular, including, such as
to define cause and effect	as a result, for this reason, because, so, therefore, consequently
to establish sequence	after, as soon as, before, finally, later, now, since then, until, when, while, afterward

The first sentence of the essay's second paragraph could be rewritten using a transition word.

> Pollution <u>also</u> hurts our national parks.

By simply adding the word *also*, a connection is made between the first and second paragraphs. The reader can see that even though a new topic (pollution) is being introduced, the second paragraph is building on what came before.

You could also place a transition at the end of the first paragraph.

> <u>However</u>, crowds of visitors aren't the only problem faced by our national parks.

CCSs: W.8.4, WHST.6-8.4

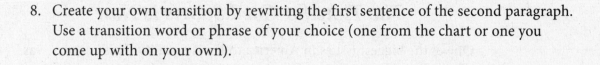

8. Create your own transition by rewriting the first sentence of the second paragraph. Use a transition word or phrase of your choice (one from the chart or one you come up with on your own).

_____

_____

Keep in mind that not all transitions use these words and phrases. For example, the first sentence of the second paragraph could also be rewritten this way:

> Just as overcrowding inside the parks can cause damage, so can the pollution that comes from outside park boundaries.

No single word or phrase marks this sentence as a transition, but the new sentence carefully links the main idea of the first paragraph (too many people in the parks) to the main idea of the second paragraph (pollution damage to the parks).

 Practice Activity 3

Directions: The essay on the next page was written in response to the question, "Should boys and girls play together on junior high and high school sports teams?" The transitions have been taken out and listed below. As you read through the essay, place the letter of the proper transition below in each of the blanks.

A. Some might argue that girls would have less choice if sports were coed because boys would take over sports that had been reserved for girls.

B. The idea of equality connects all these advantages of coed school sports teams.

C. Coed sports would not only teach equality on the field or court; they would also help teach students about equality in life.

D. The most obvious advantage of coed school sports would be that students could have a wider choice of activities in which to participate.

CCSs: W.8.4, WHST.6-8.4

The Time for Coed Sports Is Now

One of the biggest issues in America today is equality. This country was founded on the idea that all people should be given a chance to succeed at whatever they want to do. However, many barriers to true equality still exist. One example affecting young people around the country is the separation of boys' and girls' sports teams. True equality in school sports can become a reality only if all junior high and high school sports teams are open to both boys and girls.

_____ More choice in sports would mean students could participate in any athletic activity they enjoy, not just those the school system told them they could be in. Girls could play football, and boys could play volleyball. Of course, all players (boys or girls) would need the talent to actually make the team, but that's the way sports should be. Any player good enough to contribute to the team should be able to play.

_____ It's not likely, however, that all school sports teams would have only boys on them if we got rid of "boys' teams" and "girls' teams." The belief that all boys are automatically better at sports than all girls is just wrong. Sure, it helps to be taller and stronger than your opponent when playing sports, and it's true that by high school, the average boy is a few inches taller and a few pounds heavier than the average girl. Yet what really makes an athlete good is preparation, dedication, and heart—qualities that have nothing to do with a person's gender.

_____ If school sports are supposed to teach students lessons they can use in adult life, then opening up all sports teams to boys and girls can only help. Let's face it: School sports teams may not be coed now, but the real world is. There's no such thing as a "women's office" or a "men's factory." These days, men and women work together in almost every type of job. Wouldn't it help to have boys and girls learning to work together as teammates on sports teams when they're young? Isn't it time school sports caught up to the rest of the world?

_____ Coed sports would help strengthen equality by allowing all students to participate in the sport of their choice, by allowing athletes to be judged as individuals rather than simply as girls and boys, and by preparing young people to join the working world. If our country really believes in equality, we should practice it in our schools, not just read about it in textbooks. Opening up all sports to both boys and girls would be a good first step.

CCSs: W.8.4, WHST.6-8.4

One Last Thing

You're about to write a first draft of a paper. Here are a few questions you should ask yourself as you work.

- Does the writing have a clear focus?

- Is the main idea adequately supported by relevant details, reasons, examples, facts, and so on?

- Are the ideas well organized and developed, with an effective beginning, middle, and end?

- Are the ideas well suited to the specific audience and purpose?

- Is my voice appropriate for the topic, audience, and purpose?

- Does the writing use a variety of sentence structures?

- Does the writing use a variety of specific words?

- Do the sentences and paragraphs flow together and sound natural?

Lesson Practice begins on the following page.

Drafting

Use your plan from pages 127–128 to draft an essay about your favorite summertime activity on the following pages.

Writer's Checklist

✓ **A well-written draft:**

☐ shows logical organization.

☐ has a clear purpose.

☐ has a topic sentence, body, and conclusion.

☐ includes developed ideas.

☐ includes transitions between ideas.

☐ is appropriate for the audience.

Directions: Write your draft on the lines below.

_____

_____

_____

_____

_____

_____

_____

_____

_____

_____

_____

_____

_____

_____

_____

_____

_____

CCSs: W.8.5, WHST.6-8.5

Lesson 11: Revising and Editing

You want your readers to understand what you are writing. In order to make that happen, you need to be consistent and focused. Bouncing around will just confuse your reader. The tips in this lesson will help revise your writing. When you revise, you'll make your writing stronger.

 TIP 1: Maintain a consistent point of view.

As you've seen, good writing should include a variety of words and sentences. But one area in which you don't want a lot of variety is your point of view.

In Lesson 5, you learned about the different kinds of point of view. Skipping back and forth between different points of view can make a story very hard to follow. For example, it would confuse a reader if you began a story like this:

> As she hurried up the dark, lonely road toward the castle, she heard the distant rumble of thunder. Within a few minutes, as I got closer to the castle, I felt the first drops of rain sting my face.

Who is telling the story? If the author switches the point of view, it's hard to tell.

Point-of-view problems can come up in any sort of writing, not just in stories. Look at the following example of another common point-of-view error.

> When I was in the Rocky Mountains, you could really tell you were at a high altitude.

This sentence begins in the first person ("When I was . . .") but shifts in the middle to second person ("you could really tell . . ."). The writer should have kept the point of view consistent to make the meaning of the sentence clearer.

1. Rewrite the sentence to correct the point-of-view error.

_____

_____

Whose Point of View?

Some novel writers choose to change the point of view with the start of each chapter. For example, one character might narrate Chapter 1, and her best friend might narrate Chapter 2. Writers do this in an obvious, deliberate way that is clear—not confusing—to the reader.

More Consistency Concerns

Number, tense, voice, and attitude are four other areas where you need to check your work for consistency.

 TIP 2: Nouns, pronouns, and verbs should agree and may be singular or plural.

Nouns, pronouns, and verbs have numbers. In other words, they have singular and plural forms. When you shift between singular and plural nouns, pronouns, and verbs, your readers must work hard to figure out who is doing what in your writing. Remember, a **pronoun** is a word that takes the place of a noun. Pronouns include words such as *we*, *you*, *it*, *him*, *her*, *they*, and *me*.

> Any student who wants to run for student council president needs to be nominated by their classmates.

The plural pronoun *their* doesn't agree in number with the singular subject *student*. Both the pronoun and the noun it refers to must be either singular or plural.

2. Rewrite the sentence to correct this error.

_____

_____

A Note about *Their*

Some people use *their* as a shortcut when the person in question could be a male or a female. However, this usage is not grammatically correct and should be avoided.

CCSs: W.8.5, WHST.6-8.5

 TIP 3: Keep verb tenses the same.

Another common consistency error is to use different verb tenses together. Mixing past-tense, present-tense, and future-tense verbs is a sure way to confuse and distract a reader.

> The tickets for the movie were expensive, and once we will get inside, we have to spend even more for popcorn and soda.

The sentence starts out in the past tense but suddenly shifts to the future and then to the present. Although the sentence may still get its point across, it does so in an awkward and confusing way.

3. Rewrite the sentence to make the verb tenses consistent.

    _____

    _____

    _____

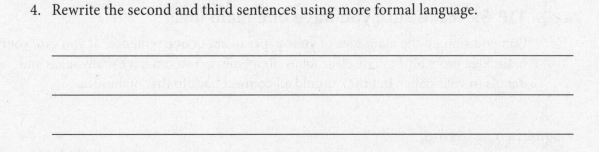 **TIP 4: Do not mix formal and informal language.**

Mixing formal and informal language is distracting to readers because it disrupts your writing voice. Switching between formal and informal language may also leave your readers wondering who is speaking. Once you have decided on the most appropriate voice for your writing, make sure you use it all the way through.

> Once the race had ended, Maribel collapsed in a heap on the grass, exhausted by the struggle of competition and the relentless heat of the blazing sun. Boy! Was she wiped, or what?

The passage begins with formal language (the kind you might use when writing an assignment for school), but ends with a sentence that sounds more like the way you would talk to friends. Mixing formal and informal language makes it harder for the reader to focus on what's being said.

4. Rewrite the second and third sentences using more formal language.

    _____

    _____

    _____

CCSs: W.8.5, WHST.6-8.5

 ## TIP 5: Check the logic of your organization.

As you read your draft, think about the best order for your paragraphs. Imagine you are reading it for the first time. Is there certain information that must come first in order for the reader to understand other information? Are there events that need to happen to a character in order for the reader to understand his or her actions?

Practice Activity 1

Directions: Put the following events in a logical order by placing numbers 1–5 in the blanks beside each sentence. Then explain why you chose the order you did.

_____ A. He took off his shoes and walked into the family room, and that's when he noticed his television was missing.

_____ B. Tim raked up the leaves in the front yard, and then went inside to watch the Fighting Irish play on the ESPN.

_____ C. Tim's favorite season is fall; he loves the colors and the cool weather.

_____ D. But most of all, Tim loves football. In college, he was a running back who played for Notre Dame.

_____ E. These days, Tim spends more time on his own grass than on the football field, and this afternoon was like most Saturdays.

Explain why you chose the order you did.

_____

_____

_____

_____

 ## TIP 6: Make sure you have one main idea.

Can you sum up the main idea of your paper in about one sentence? If you can, your main idea probably has one clear focus. Remember: You can have many ideas and details in your paper, but they should all connect back to that main idea.

CCSs: W.8.5, WHST.6-8.5

 ## TIP 7: Check that all your paragraphs connect to your main idea.

As you reread each paragraph, ask yourself if it explains or supports your main idea. All writing should have one main focus. If there are paragraphs or sentences that discuss topics that don't come back to the main idea, they probably don't belong.

 ## TIP 8: Make sure you have enough detail for your reader to understand your writing.

Remember that not everyone who reads your writing will know how you came up with an idea or know the background information that supports your ideas. As you read each paragraph, think of questions a reader might have about your information. Then, try to answer those questions by adding details to the paragraph.

 ## TIP 9: Make sure each paragraph is completely developed.

Remember that every paragraph needs a topic sentence, a few sentences or more in the body of the paragraph, and a concluding sentence. As you read your draft, underline your topic sentences in each paragraph. Then check to see that each sentence connects back to the topic sentence.

Read the following paragraph, then complete Numbers 5 and 6.

> The bulk bins at the natural food store were overflowing with good foods to snack on. Jasmine was having trouble making up her mind. She really loved the honey-roasted almonds in the new trail mix, but she wanted to try something new. She walked to the end of the row and found a bin with dried fruit. There were cranberries, apples, and apricots all mixed together in one. "The only things missing are some almonds," she thought. Jasmine scooted back to the middle of the row and spied the nut mix. The bin was filled with sunflower seeds, pumpkin seeds, cashews, and almonds. "There," she whispered to herself. "That's what I want."

5. Underline the topic sentence in the above paragraph.

6. On the lines below, write down the details that support the topic sentence.

_____

_____

_____

TIP 10: Read your draft for style, tone, and word choice.

Think about your audience when deciding on your style, tone, and word choice. Do you need to sound serious or humorous? Should your language be formal or informal? Are the words you're using specific enough and understandable to a reader who might be unfamiliar with your topic?

Word choice is also important for concrete details. Make sure your words are specific so that your reader knows exactly what you mean. For example, instead of saying "Charlie took the book from Ben," you could say, "Charlie grabbed the science textbook from Ben." The second sentence helps the reader better imagine what's happening.

 Practice Activity 2

Directions: Choose a specific word or phrase to replace the more general word that is underlined in each sentence. Write your answer on the line.

1. Antoinette threw the <u>ball</u>.

    _____

2. My family always <u>takes a vacation</u>.

    _____

3. Celia's new phone is <u>pretty amazing</u>.

    _____

4. The Web site gives you <u>information</u>.

    _____

5. An <u>animal</u> jumped onto my car in the middle of traffic.

    _____

CCSs: W.8.5, WHST.6-8.5

 TIP 11: Have someone else read your draft.

Sometimes you need distance from your writing to see it clearly, and occasionally you need a whole new set of eyes. Having someone else look at your writing will help you identify things that need to be fixed, like weak transitions or underdeveloped ideas. If you're at home, you can ask a family member or friend to take a look at your paper.

At school, your teacher may have you conduct a peer review by swapping papers with a classmate. You will read and provide feedback on each other's writing. Remember that the feedback you provide should be constructive, or helpful. Avoid using negative comments and put-downs. While the goal of a peer review is to give your classmate useful ideas to improve his or her writing, you can also point out what he or she has already done well in the paper. Peer reviews give you an extra chance to practice revising, and you'll have a better idea of how you can improve your own work!

 TIP 12: Don't be afraid to try a new approach.

If, you've spent time revising your writing, and you feel like it still isn't making the point you'd like it to make, consider a new approach. Rethink your purpose and your audience. Is there another format that would work better? Perhaps you're writing in short story form when an essay might work better, or vice versa. Writing is a creative exercise; be open to trying new or different approaches until you find the one that best fits your purpose.

Lesson Practice begins on the following page.

Revising and Editing

Read through the essay draft you wrote on pages 126 and 127. Revise and edit your draft. Write your final copy on the following pages.

Writer's Checklist

✔ **A well-written essay:**

- ☐ shows logical organization.
- ☐ includes developed ideas.
- ☐ has a clear purpose.
- ☐ has one main idea.
- ☐ is appropriate for the audience.
- ☐ includes transitions between ideas and paragraphs.
- ☐ features correct grammar and sentence structure.
- ☐ maintains a consistent point of view and style.

Directions: Write your final copy on the lines below.

_____

_____

_____

_____

_____

_____

_____

_____

_____

_____

_____

_____

_____

_____

_____

_____

_____

_____

CCSs: W.8.1a, WHST.6-8.1a

Lesson 12: Writing Arguments

Sometimes, you need to persuade others to share your views or take a specific action. You'll need to make a logical argument. So how do you do that? Read on.

TIP 1: Take a position worth arguing.

You can't have an argument about something if everyone agrees. There's no argument over most scientific facts, for example. You can argue that the sun rises in the west and sets in the east if you want, but most people won't bother to listen to you. So, when you write an argument, pick a subject about which there is some disagreement.

Likewise, certain opinions are widely agreed upon. Most people would agree that exercise leads to a healthy life, for example, and they won't be too interested in another person's thoughts on the matter. But if you can present an argument for the best way to exercise, you're off to a good start.

TIP 2: Clearly state your position.

Once you have your position, make sure that it is narrow enough to cover in an essay. Let's say that you decided to write your essay about exercise. It could take thousands of pages to cover every type of exercise. You are more likely to write an effective persuasive essay if you narrow your topic to something specific. For example, instead of the broad topic "exercise is good," you could narrow it to "walking 30 minutes a day is essential for good health."

Then, when you have your specific topic, make sure that you state your position clearly so that the reader understands what your argument will be.

Read the following statement.

> The beach is a great place.

That's a very broad statement! You will need to narrow your focus. What is great about it? The scenery? The activities you can do there? The sea life?

1. Write a more specific statement that narrows the topic.

_____

_____

TIP 3: Support your position with facts and evidence.

The phone rings. Your mother answers, and a voice says, "I saw your son cheat on a test yesterday afternoon." Your mother says, "How do you know he cheated?" The caller says, "He did. Take my word for it." Would your mother believe such an accusation against you? We hope not. We hope she would ask for evidence.

When you are trying to persuade a reader to agree with something, saying "take my word for it" isn't enough either. You need to provide evidence to back up what you say.

The best evidence is factual—things people can look up and see for themselves. Testimony from experts is another strong type of evidence.

Let's go back to the topic of exercise. This is your position on the issue:

> Walking 30 minutes a day is essential for good health.

Here is your argument, which is the case you make for doing what you recommend:

> Because it helps people manage their weight and prevent diseases.

Now, support that argument with factual testimony:

> Researchers found that 30 minutes of cardio exercise a day, such as walking, and switching to a healthier diet dropped health risks dramatically in just 6 weeks. Risks for killers such as diabetes, cancer, and heart disease were greatly reduced, according to a study by Brigham Young University professor of exercise science Steven Aldana, published in the Journal of the American Dietetic Association, March 2005.

2. What type of facts and evidence would you need to back up the specific position you wrote in Number 1? List them on the following lines.

_____

_____

_____

_____

_____

_____

CCSs: W.8.1b, WHST.6-8.1a

 TIP 4: Address counterarguments.

Any issue worth arguing has two or more sides. An effective way to persuade people to adopt your point of view is to address the other side and explain why that side is incorrect.

> Counterargument: Exercise can cause other problems that offset its good, like foot problems, weak knees, and back pain.

> Response to counterargument: These problems can be minimized by using the proper equipment—quality shoes, knee braces, and so on.

3. Imagine that an advertisement for Burger World urges, "Try Burger World's new Double Super French Fried Bacon Cheeseburger today! It's the biggest, tastiest, longest-named burger on Earth!" What is a counterargument you could offer to this position?

_____

_____

 TIP 5: Organize your writing carefully.

Organization is important in any piece of writing. Make sure your facts and evidence are presented in an effective order. Sometimes that may mean putting the strongest evidence first; other times, the strongest evidence may be more effective at the end. Remember to use good transitions to connect them. At the very end, sum up your evidence and restate your original position.

Your facts and evidence can be organized in various ways. Here is a short list of a few of the ways you can organize a persuasive essay or letter.

- **Pros and cons**—Present one side of the argument and then counter it with the arguments on the other side.

- **Cause and effect**—When you organize your argument in this way, you show how one event or reason leads to another result, which leads to another, and so on.

- **Parody**—Represent the other side in a humorous way, such as in an editorial cartoon.

TIP 6: Tell your ideas in an order that makes sense.

As you learned in Lesson 10, transitions help the reader understand how your ideas fit together to support your topic. Transitions will help your reader see the relationships between your ideas. Some transitions, such as *also*, *in the same way*, *similarly*, and *likewise*, can be used to indicate that the idea you are introducing is similar to one that came before. Others, such as *although*, *despite*, *even though*, *however*, *yet*, and *on the other hand*, can be used to introduce a contrasting idea. Get to know different transitions and their uses.

Read this paragraph, then answer Numbers 4 and 5.

> (1) The speaker in Walt Whitman's poem "Song of Myself" really enjoys being himself. (2) He enjoys himself so much that he begins the poem by declaring, "I celebrate myself, and sing myself." (3) He takes pleasure in being alive. (4) He can just sit and look at a blade of grass. (5) His enjoyment of himself is so intense that he feels connected to everything. (6) He describes his tongue and every atom of his blood as "form'd from this soil, this air." (7) It is as though he is very big and consists of everything.

4. Where would the following sentence best fit in the paragraph?

   He also says that he hopes "to cease not till death," which means that he hopes that his health and vitality will last.

   A. after sentence 1
   B. after sentence 2
   C. after sentence 4
   D. after sentence 7

5. Which of the following is the best way to revise sentence 4?

   A. Finally, he can just sit and look at a blade of grass.
   B. On the other hand, he can just sit and look at a blade of grass.
   C. For example, he can just sit and look at a blade of grass.
   D. To conclude, he can just sit and look at a blade of grass.

There are many ways of showing connections between ideas and sentences. Refer to the chart on page 138 for a list of transition words and their connections.

CCSs: W.8.1d, W.8.1e, WHST.6-8.1d, WHST.6-8.1e

 TIP 7: Remember to use an objective style and a neutral tone.

In order to best persuade your readers, you must present yourself as not only knowledgeable, but also objective and fair. Consider the following arguments.

Argument 1: Without 30 minutes of walking each day, this nation is going to be full of people who are overweight and disgusting. There is no excuse for not exercising; the only reason people don't participate is because they are lazy.

Argument 2: Thirty minutes of walking a day has proven to fight obesity and lead to a healthier lifestyle. While we all have busy lives, we should all try to make time for this important activity. The benefits far outweigh any excuses.

6. With which argument would you most likely agree? Why?

_____

_____

 TIP 8: Include a strong concluding statement.

Like a lawyer in a courtroom, you have gathered the evidence and presented your case; now its time for your closing argument.

Your concluding statement should tie up your strongest arguments with your main idea. This is your last chance to persuade your audience, so you do not want to end abruptly or weakly. For instance, consider this conclusion for the essay on exercise:

Anyone can carve out 30 minutes each day. It's easy.

This statement doesn't say very much. It could be stronger. Compare it to this statement:

The benefits of walking 30 minutes a day far outweigh the risks, so take the necessary steps toward a healthier you.

This statement sums up the argument, reminding the reader of its main points while leaving the reader with something to think about.

Lesson Practice begins on the following page.

Directions: Read the following article about cell phones in schools. Then respond to the writing prompt.

Education in the Information Age

by Janessa Lucas

The debate over allowing cell phones in school has heated up in the past few years and shows no signs of dying. We live in an age where people expect to be constantly in contact, and cell phones are one way to accomplish this. With the popularity of smart phones, people have come to rely on having a phone and Internet-ready device in their hands at all times. As more and more young people own cell phones, we are forced to ask the question: is it possible to be *too* connected, and where do we draw the line? Allowing cell phones in schools has moved to the forefront of this debate.

Those in favor of allowing cell phones in schools point to the following:

- Having cell phones in school would allow students to text missed assignments to friends who are sick and missing school.

- Most cell phones come equipped with calculators that students could use for math.

- Students who are slow at writing down notes can take pictures of the board. This way, they won't miss any of the notes the teacher has written down.

- In the event of an emergency, students could reach their parents immediately.

- Cell phones are convenient. If students are allowed to bring them to school, parents would be able to text or call their kids whenever they need to.

Those opposed to allowing cell phones in school cite these reasons:

- Cell phones would provide an easy way to cheat, as students could text test answers to their friends.

- Cell phones are disruptive. Students may forget to turn them off, leading to distractions during class.

- The long-term effects of cell phones are still unknown. It could be hazardous to young people's health to allow extended use of cell phones.

- In the event of a real emergency, cell phone usage could overwhelm communication channels.

- Cell phones haven't been allowed in schools in years past. Students didn't need them then, and they don't need them now.

Argument Writing Prompt

Write an argument for or against allowing cell phones in school. Plan your essay on the following page. Write your final essay on pages 163 and 164.

Writer's Checklist

✔ **A well-written argument:**

☐ introduces a claim.

☐ supports the claim with clear reasons and relevant evidence.

☐ conveys the relationships among claims and reasons.

☐ sustains an objective style and tone.

☐ provides a concluding statement.

Directions: Plan your argument in the space below.

Directions: Write your argument on the lines below.

_____

_____

_____

_____

_____

_____

_____

_____

_____

_____

_____

_____

_____

_____

_____

_____

_____

_____

_____

_____

_____

_____

_____

_____

_____

_____

_____

_____

_____

_____

_____

_____

_____

_____

CCSs: W.8.2a, W.8.2b, WHST.6-8.2a, WHST.6-8.2b

Lesson 13: Writing Informative Texts

The purpose of informational writing is to explain, define, or instruct. When you write an informational piece, you act as a teacher. You pass along information to someone who might not know what you know. Your goal is to share information with others in a way that's easy for them to understand.

 ## TIP 1: Establish a main idea.

Whether you're writing a report about the Navajo tribe of the American southwest, an essay about hip-hop music, or an article about an inspiring person, your basic purpose is the same: to provide information, clearly and accurately. To do this, you need to have a main idea. Trying to write about the Navajo tribe as a whole is too much; you need to narrow your focus to something like the language of the Navajo tribe or their cultural practices. All of your writing should focus on supporting this main idea.

 ## TIP 2: Present the information as clearly as possible.

When writing an informational essay, you are presenting information to your audience. Remember that your reader may not know as much about your topic as you do. It's important to present the information as clearly and carefully as you can. Think about what your readers might need to know in order to understand your topic and be sure to include those details. Concentrate on writing an effective beginning, middle, and end.

 ## TIP 3: Only present relevant information.

Don't include anything that doesn't relate to the main topic of your own paper. Part of your prewriting task will be to organize all of the information that you already know about the topic. You may need to read articles on your subject and decide which parts of each book or article relate to the focus of your paper. You must sort through the resources and pick out information that is relevant.

 ## TIP 4: Maintain a formal style.

Informative texts are usually formal types of writing. As such, you should maintain a formal style throughout. Avoid casual or overly familiar language, such as slang. The purpose of an informative text is to educate your audience. Informal or casual language is better saved for narratives or letters.

CCSs: W.8.2a, W.8.2b, W.8.2c, WHST.6-8.2a, WHST.6-8.2b, WHST.6-8.2c

 TIP 5: **Include cause–and–effect relationships when appropriate.**

Analyzing cause and effect is an excellent way to explain why something happened or to show the consequences of some event or situation.

To analyze why something has happened, state the effect and analyze its cause or causes.

Effect	Causes
People communicate with one another constantly.	Most people own cell phones.
	Computer (e-mail) use is part of daily life.
	Communication gadgets are "in."

To analyze the consequences of some event or situation, state the cause and analyze its effect or what results it creates.

Cause	Effects
Eighth graders in my school started writing in all subject areas.	Writing test scores have increased.
	Students are less afraid to write.
	Students are exposed to a variety of writing forms.

TIP 6: **Describe a problem and offer a solution.**

Problem and solution papers try to explain how to solve a problem. In most cases, problem and solution papers discuss a problem that relates to many people. You may discuss traffic congestion in a certain area of your town and offer suggestions for how to fix the problem. It may be something global, like the problem of the polar ice caps melting and what kinds of solutions people across the world might use to help remedy the problem.

When you are offering solutions to the problem, make sure they are relevant. Your suggestions for solutions should be connected to the information you describe in the problem.

Cause-and-Effect Words and Phrases

because	consequently
therefore	a result
so	for this reason

(Many of these can be used for problem and solution, as well.)

CCSs: W.8.2a, W.8.2b, W.8.2c, W.8.2d, W.8.2e, WHST.6-8.2a, WHST.6-8.2b, WHST.6-8.2c, WHST.6-8.2e

 TIP 7: Compare and contrast two different ideas or subjects.

In papers that compare and contrast, the writer presents two or more things that are alike and different. For example, an article about European football (also known as soccer) and American football might be organized to discuss the similarities between the two sports, then the differences.

Use what you know about the different ways of writing informational texts to answer Number 1.

1. Read this topic sentence from an informational essay.

   Abebe Bikila and Jeff Blatnik each faced seemingly insurmountable obstacles on the road to becoming Olympic gold medalists.

   How would you organize this essay? Why?

   _____

   _____

   _____

 TIP 8: Don't just tell your readers—show them.

Be descriptive in every type of writing. Use details that appeal to the reader's senses (sight, hearing, taste, touch, and smell). Your writing will leave a lasting impression if you use descriptions that help the reader experience your point first-hand.

Compare-and-Contrast Words and Phrases	
also	similarly
as	likewise
but	even though
although	yet
despite	on the other hand
however	otherwise
instead	in the same way

CCSs: W.8.2b, WHST.6-8.2a, WHST.6-8.2d

The sentences below show how one student revised part of his paper by adding more details.

First Draft: The school halls are too crowded.

Final Paper: In between classes at my school, the hallway is packed with students who are slammed next to each other, shuffling along in an endless swarm.

Now you try. Read the following sentence, then complete Number 2.

Graffiti is a major problem in our community.

2. Rewrite this sentence with descriptive details.

_____

_____

_____

_____

 TIP 9: Use graphs, charts, tables, and/or maps to illustrate your information.

It can be very helpful to your reader to see a visual of the information you are presenting. Information about a change over time can sometimes be understood more clearly by looking at the changes in a line graph or chart. Look at the following example of a student's report on her homeroom's favorite ice cream flavors.

Flavors	Boys	Girls
vanilla	3	2
chocolate	5	7
strawberry	0	2
pistachio	2	4

The questionnaire given to students shows that most prefer chocolate ice cream over vanilla. It also shows that more girls than boys like chocolate. What was surprising was the number of students who chose pistachio ice cream as their favorite.

CCSs: W.8.2b, WHST.6-8.2a, WHST.6-8.2b, WHST.6-8.2c, WHST.6-8.2d, WHST.6-8.2e, WHST.6-8.2f

 TIP 10: Use primary and secondary sources.

If you are asked to use sources for a writing assignment, remember that not all sources are alike. Some sources have errors or misleading information. This is especially true for Internet sites. Using more than one site helps you make sure that your information is correct.

As you learned in Lesson 7, a **primary source** is a document or other source of information created by people who were directly involved with the topic. Examples include speeches, autobiographies, photographs, interviews with eyewitnesses, and live recordings. A **secondary source** is a document or other source of information created by people who were not directly involved with the topic. Examples include textbooks, encyclopedia articles, essays, and reports.

You cannot just copy information from a book or an article and present it as if it were your own. Paraphrase or restate the ideas in your own words. You also cannot use specific ideas from other sources without saying where they came from. There are many ways of crediting your sources. Most include putting a list at the end of your essay that has the titles and authors of the books or articles you used, along with the page numbers where the information was found. Here is part of a list of sources for a paper about the Great Wall of China.

> Forrester, Dean. *The History of China*. New York: Nottingmer Publishing Company, 1995, pp. 34–41.

> Montz, Julia. "The Great Wall of China: Attracting Visitors for Centuries." *Today's Tourist*, Sept. 1998, pp. 12–14.

 TIP 11: Whichever form your writing takes, remember a few basic guidelines.

1. Clearly establish the purpose or main point of your paper and how you will address the topic.

2. Choose the most important supporting facts or ideas about your topic and write only about these ideas.

3. Organize the ideas and supporting details in a logical way so that your paper flows easily from point to point.

4. Write clearly so that someone not familiar with the subject will understand you.

5. Conclude by summing up the ideas of your essay in an interesting way that ties the paper together.

Lesson Practice begins on the following page.

Informational Writing Prompt

Write an informational essay about a person you admire. This may be a famous person, such as your favorite author or sports star, or someone less well known, such as a family member. Plan your essay on the following page. Write your final essay on pages 172 and 173.

Writer's Checklist

✓ **A well-written essay:**

☐ establishes a main idea.

☐ presents information as clearly as possible.

☐ only presents relevant information.

☐ maintains a formal style and tone.

☐ is descriptive.

☐ uses reliable sources.

Directions: Plan your essay in the space below.

Directions: Write your essay on the lines below.

_____

_____

_____

_____

_____

_____

_____

_____

_____

_____

_____

_____

_____

_____

_____

_____

_____

_____

_____

_____

_____

_____

_____

_____

_____

_____

_____

_____

_____

_____

_____

_____

_____

_____

_____

_____

_____

_____

_____

CCSs: W.8.3a, W.8.3b

Lesson 14: Writing Narratives

Narrative writing includes stories, poems, songs, and plays. There are many skills you can practice through narrative writing that will help you with your expository, informational, and persuasive writing.

When you write a narrative, you are acting as a storyteller. Even though there are many ways in which to write a story, they all have common elements. Your story needs to have a plot, at least one character, and a setting for the action. A story also needs a point of view and a narrator. Here are a few tips to consider when planning and writing a narrative, whether it is true or made up.

TIP 1: Describe your character(s).

Readers want the writer to tell them how characters look, sound, think, and feel. Details might include a character's physical features (such as height and hairstyle), clothing, habits, likes, dislikes, and so on. If your story has more than one character, make them different enough so that the reader can tell them apart by their actions as well as their words.

A **complex character** is one who displays more than one personality trait. For example, a short story might feature a character who is genuinely good at heart, but doesn't always do good things. Take, for example, the story of Robin Hood. Robin Hood breaks the law and defies his king by stealing from the rich and giving to the poor, but you can argue that his actions are just. He is a complex character.

On the other hand, a character that is all evil or all good is not complex. We don't encounter very many one-dimensional people in real life, so we shouldn't in fiction either. Any narrative you write should include at least one complex character.

TIP 2: Describe a clear setting for the action.

A story's setting is when and where the action takes place. Details about the setting should include information about time of day or night, weather, landscape, buildings, and so on. Is the action taking place now, a hundred years ago, or two thousand years in the future? Make sure you give the reader a good idea about where and when the action is taking place.

1. Imagine that you have been asked to write a story about an eighth-grade student who has traveled back in time. Describe the setting of his or her adventure on the line below.

_____

TIP 3: Create an organized plot with conflict.

The plot is the series of related events that make up a story. A plot is usually organized in sequential order, with one event leading to the next.

Most plots are based on conflicts. A **conflict** is a problem faced by a character. Characters may have conflicts with other characters, society, nature, or even themselves.

If you can keep your characters working to solve problems, your readers will stay interested. Maybe your character is stranded on a distant planet, lost in a deep jungle, struggling to win a baseball championship, or building a secret hideaway. Just make sure the character is challenged by his or her situation. These problems or conflicts will become the story's plot. You can use a story map to help you plan the plot. (You learned about story maps in Lesson 9.)

You may also use one of the following plot devices to add interest to your stories.

Plot Device	Description
flashback	A flashback occurs when the author pauses in the story to describe events that happened in the past. These past events help the reader better understand what is going on in the story's present. A flashback may be as short as a paragraph or may continue for several pages. Consider the story about a character trapped on a distant planet. A flashback could show how the character ended up there.
flash forward	This is the opposite of a flashback. A flash forward occurs when the author describes events and elements of the future. These future events add meaning to what is happening in the present. A flash forward in your space story could show the main character's death or thrilling escape from the mystery planet. Knowing what is coming will add a layer of suspense for your readers.
subplot	A subplot supports the main plot. It may focus on things like two characters' relationship to one another, or a minor character's story. Subplots are not essential to the main story, but they add an interesting layer. Remember the movie *Up*? In it, a young boy and an old man find adventure by flying a house to South America. Throughout the course of the movie, it becomes apparent that the young boy does not have much of a relationship with his own father. This is a subplot.

No matter which plot devices you use, it is important to provide a resolution to your plot. The **resolution** is the outcome of the action or conflict. A character stranded on a distant planet or lost in a jungle must either find his way home or make a new home on the foreign planet. Likewise, it would not be very rewarding to read a story about a team struggling to win a baseball championship without finding out what happens when they get to the championship. Make sure your plot comes to a logical conclusion.

 ## TIP 4: Choose a point of view.

When you write a fictional story, you need to choose a point of view. Remember, point of view refers to what kind of narrator a story has. If the story is told in the first-person point of view, the narrator is a character in the story and uses words like *I*, *myself*, and *we*. If the story is told in the third-person point of view, the narrator is not part of the story and uses words like *he*, *she*, and *they*. Whichever point of view you choose, you should be consistent.

When you write a personal narrative, you don't need to decide on a point of view. A personal narrative is a true story about your life. Personal narratives are almost always told from the point of view of the author.

 ## TIP 5: Give physical details through your characters' senses.

As the action progresses, let the reader know what the characters see, hear, and feel. In some stories, you may even want your characters to describe what they taste or smell.

2. Think about the time-traveling eighth grader from Number 1. What would he or she experience during this trip into history? Write down one detail relating to each of the five senses.

Sense	Description
sight	
sound	
smell	
taste	
touch	

CCSs: W.8.3a, W.8.3b, W.8.3c, W.8.3d

 ## TIP 6: Let characters speak their own words.

Dialogue is the part of a story in which the characters speak out loud. When writing dialogue, the following rules are helpful.

There are three ways to tell the reader who is speaking:

- Before the quote

  She said, "No! I won't eat broccoli-ripple ice cream."

- In the middle of the quote

  "No!" she said. "I won't eat broccoli-ripple ice cream."

- After the quote

  "No! I won't eat broccoli-ripple ice cream," she said.

Remember that commas and periods always go inside the quotation marks. Begin a new paragraph whenever a speaker finishes. Also, make sure the dialogue sounds realistic. You might find it helpful to whisper your characters' words to yourself as you write.

 ## TIP 7: Use figurative language to make your writing more interesting.

In Lesson 4, you learned about figurative language. Figurative language is used to create vivid pictures in readers' minds. Writing that uses figurative language means something other than what it says. It goes beyond the literal or dictionary meanings of words. The metaphor "Riley is a bolt of lightning on the track" does not mean that Riley is lightning. It just means that Riley is a very fast runner.

When writing short stories, poems, and other kinds of narrative writing, be sure to use figurative language. It will spice up your writing by expressing your ideas in interesting and unusual ways.

 ## TIP 8: Write about real-life events.

Narrative writing can be completely made up, but it can also be about things that have happened in real life. You can write a story about what happened at school yesterday using all the elements discussed in this lesson. Instead of writing about fictional characters, write about people you know. Instead of planning a plot, describe the most interesting events you or your family members have experienced. You can even use dialogue and figurative language to bring your true story to life.

CCSs: W.8.3a, W.8.3b, W.8.3c, W.8.3d

 ## TIP 9: Use details and information to add interest to your story.

To make your story more exciting, you may want to add expository writing to your narrative. **Expository writing** is writing that gives your reader information or explains something.

Imagine you are writing a true story about your uncle's farm. In order to make the story more interesting and believable, you would want to talk about the kinds of animals on his farm, or what happened when a tornado touched down in one of his fields. Expository writing can provide facts or give details about an aspect of your story.

You may need to do some research to make sure you get your facts straight. Research could mean searching the Internet for information about farms. You could also interview your uncle about what happened during the tornado. Research like this can be helpful when you don't know all the details about a true story.

Even if your story is fictional, you can add expository elements to it to make it more suspenseful and interesting. The novel *Hatchet* by Gary Paulsen is about a boy named Brian who survives a plane crash only to find himself alone in the Canadian wilderness. Even though it is a fictional story, Paulsen includes many factual details about surviving in the wilderness. These details make *Hatchet* a thrilling read.

 ## TIP 10: Use expository writing to talk about ideas.

Good stories have plots, conflicts, settings, and well-developed characters. They may also talk about ideas of interest to the author. A story about an alien invasion of Earth may also contain writing about war and technology. As a writer, you are free to include and explain your ideas about anything that is relevant to your story.

On a writing test, you may be asked to write about your ideas or opinions on a topic. You may want to use a mix of expository and narrative writing to do this. For example, imagine you are asked to explain why education is important. You can write a narrative story about your own education, or the education of someone you know. Then you can use expository writing to explain why the story you have written shows the importance of education.

CCSs: W.8.3a, W.8.3b, W.8.3c, W.8.3d

 Practice Activity

Directions: Read the following sentences.

The boy couldn't believe his luck. He was just handed a box to open. What would happen next would change his life.

Write a story about the boy, the box, and what happens next.

_____

_____

_____

_____

_____

_____

_____

_____

_____

_____

_____

_____

_____

Lesson Practice begins on the following page.

Narrative Writing Prompt

Write a narrative about a character trying to throw a surprise party for a friend or family member. Plan your narrative on the following page. Write your final narrative on pages 182 and 183.

Writer's Checklist

✓ **A well-written narrative:**

☐ has vivid characters.

☐ has a clear setting.

☐ has an organized plot with a logical resolution.

☐ maintains consistent point of view.

☐ uses figurative language.

☐ uses details and facts to add interest.

Practice | **181**

Directions: Plan your narrative in the space below.

Directions: Write your narrative on the lines below.

CCSs: RI.8.10, W.8.9, WHST.6-8.9

Lesson 15: Writing a Response to Reading

Writing an essay that responds to a work of literature adds a twist to the ordinary writing assignment: You must use your reading skills as well as your writing skill by describing, explaining, or reacting to the main points of a passage in your own words. This lesson will walk you through the process of planning and writing a response to literature.

 TIP 1: Figure out what kind of response the assignment is asking for.

In Lesson 4, you learned to identify the author's purpose, which is usually to inform, describe, entertain, or persuade. Like any other author, you need to understand your reason for writing. You also need to keep your readers in mind and have a sense of what they are looking for.

Luckily, when you are writing a response essay, your purpose for writing and the needs of your audience are hardly mysterious. The writing prompt itself describes your purpose and exactly what your audience is looking for! A response item might ask you to explain a process. Or, it might ask you to describe similarities and differences. Look for verbs in the question or prompt, and see what those verbs are specifically asking you to do.

Read these stanzas from "Song of Myself," a poem by Walt Whitman.

> I celebrate myself, and sing myself,
> And what I assume you shall assume,
> For every atom belonging to me as good belongs to you.
>
> I loafe and invite my soul,
> I lean and loafe at my ease observing a spear of summer grass.
>
> My tongue, every atom of my blood, form'd from this soil, this air,
> Born here of parents born here from parents the same, and their parents the same,
> I, now thirty-seven years old in perfect health begin,
> Hoping to cease not till death.

Consider this writing prompt and answer the questions on the next page.

> Write an essay in which you describe the speaker's attitude toward himself in "Song of Myself." Support your answer with details from the poem.

CCSs: RI.8.10, W.8.9, WHST.6-8.9

1. What would be your purpose in writing an essay in response to this item?

_____

_____

2. What would the audience of your essay be looking for?

_____

_____

_____

TIP 2: Make a plan.

With your purpose in mind, review the text and make a plan for your essay. Your strategy will depend on what you need to do to form a response to the item. Do you already have a sense of how you will respond to the item, but just need to collect details to use to support it? Or are you uncertain about your answer, and need to review the text with the writing prompt in mind? Use the reading skills you've practiced throughout this book to determine the main idea, note supporting details, make inferences, evaluate the author's argument, and so on.

Once you've reviewed the text and noted some of the information you'd like to use, put together a plan for your writing. To manage this stage of the writing process, it's a good idea to know what kind of writer you are. Do you like to get going by freewriting or just listing all of your ideas in no particular order? Or, maybe you like to use a graphic organizer to help you see the relationships between your ideas. Plan your response in whichever way will work best for you.

TIP 3: Think about what you've read and put those thoughts into your own words.

An assignment that asks you to write about a work of literature will usually require you to think about what you've read and put those thoughts in your own words. You might be asked to describe how the work made you feel, or to tell whether you liked the work and why. You might also be asked to explain what the work means or what the reader should get from it. But in all these cases, you're writing about your own thoughts regarding a work of literature, not just summarizing it.

TIP 4: Keep your main idea in mind as you write.

Have you ever noticed that when you're talking with friends, your conversations can take all kinds of bizarre twists and turns?

When writing a response, you want to have more control over your ideas. Planning your writing helps you to achieve this. For every paragraph and sentence you write, ask yourself: *How does this relate to my main idea?* Each paragraph should tell something specific about your main idea, and each paragraph should focus on one and only one supporting idea. If a sentence doesn't help you explain your main idea, leave it out.

 ## TIP 5: Give specific examples from the work to back up what you say about it.

Imagine that you're planning to go to the movies. Two of your friends recommend a movie to you. One friend says, "It's a great movie! You should see it!" Your other friend says, "The movie was so funny that at one point, I was wiping tears from my eyes. I was laughing that hard!" You're more likely to take the advice of the friend who backed up his recommendation with a specific reason why you should see the movie.

Similarly, your written response is simply more credible if you back it up with specific and relevant evidence from the text. Details from the work you're writing about are the supporting evidence you need to write a good essay about a work of literature.

3. Which statement from "Song of Myself" provides the best evidence that the speaker feels connected to the reader?

   A. "I celebrate myself, and sing myself …"

   B. "For every atom belonging to me as good belongs to you."

   C. "I loafe and invite my soul …"

   D. "I, now thirty-seven years old in perfect health begin …"

Lesson Practice begins on the following page.

186

Directions: Read the following excerpt from *Little Women* by Louisa May Alcott. Then respond to the writing prompt.

from

Little Women

by Louisa May Alcott

If "genius is eternal patience," as Michelangelo affirms, Amy had some claim to the divine attribute, for she persevered in spite of all obstacles, failures, and discouragements, firmly believing that in time she should do something worthy to be called "high art."

She was learning, doing, and enjoying other things, meanwhile, for she had resolved to be an attractive and accomplished woman, even if she never became a great artist. Here she succeeded better, for she was one of those happily created beings who please without effort, make friends everywhere, and take life so gracefully and easily that less fortunate souls are tempted to believe that such are born under a lucky star. Everybody liked her, for among her good gifts was tact. She had an instinctive sense of what was pleasing and proper, always said the right thing to the right person, did just what suited the time and place, and was so self-possessed that her sisters used to say, "If Amy went to court without any rehearsal beforehand, she'd know exactly what to do."

One of her weaknesses was a desire to move in "our best society," without being quite sure what the best really was. Money, position, fashionable accomplishments, and elegant manners were most desirable things in her eyes, and she liked to associate with those who possessed them, often mistaking the false for the true, and admiring what was not admirable. Never forgetting that by birth she was a gentlewoman, she cultivated her aristocratic tastes and feelings, so that when the opportunity came she might be ready to take the place from which poverty now excluded her.

"My lady," as her friends called her, sincerely desired to be a genuine lady, and was so at heart, but had yet to learn that money cannot buy refinement of nature, that rank does not always confer nobility, and that true breeding makes itself felt in spite of external drawbacks.

"I want to ask a favor of you, Mamma," Amy said, coming in with an important air one day.

"Well, little girl, what is it?" replied her mother, in whose eyes the stately young lady still remained "the baby."

"Our drawing class breaks up next week, and before the girls separate for the summer, I want to ask them out here for a day. They are wild to see the river, sketch the broken bridge, and copy some of the things they admire in my book. They have been very kind to me in many ways, and I am grateful, for they are all rich and I know I am poor, yet they never made any difference."

"Why should they?" And Mrs. March put the question with what the girls called her "Maria Theresa air."

"You know as well as I that it does make a difference with nearly everyone, so don't ruffle up like a dear, motherly hen, when your chickens get pecked by smarter birds. The ugly duckling turned out a swan, you know." And Amy smiled without bitterness, for she possessed a happy temper and hopeful spirit.

Mrs. March laughed, and smoothed down her maternal pride as she asked, "Well, my swan, what is your plan?"

"I should like to ask the girls out to lunch next week, to take them for a drive to the places they want to see, a row on the river, perhaps, and make a little artistic fete for them."

"That looks feasible. What do you want for lunch? Cake, sandwiches, fruit, and coffee will be all that is necessary, I suppose?"

"Oh, dear, no! We must have cold tongue and chicken, French chocolate and ice cream, besides. The girls are used to such things, and I want my lunch to be proper and elegant, though I do work for my living."

"How many young ladies are there?" asked her mother, beginning to look sober.

"Twelve or fourteen in the class, but I dare say they won't all come."

"Bless me, child, you will have to charter an omnibus to carry them about."

"Why, Mother, how can you think of such a thing? Not more than six or eight will probably come, so I shall hire a beach wagon and borrow Mr. Laurence's cherry-bounce." (Hannah's pronunciation of *charabanc*.)

"All of this will be expensive, Amy."

"Not very. I've calculated the cost, and I'll pay for it myself."

"Don't you think, dear, that as these girls are used to such things, and the best we can do will be nothing new, that some simpler plan would be pleasanter to them, as a change if nothing more, and much better for us than buying or borrowing what we don't need, and attempting a style not in keeping with our circumstances?"

"If I can't have it as I like, I don't care to have it at all. I know that I can carry it out perfectly well, if you and the girls will help a little, and I don't see why I can't if I'm willing to pay for it," said Amy, with the decision which opposition was apt to change into obstinacy.

Mrs. March knew that experience was an excellent teacher, and when it was possible she left her children to learn alone the lessons which she would gladly have made easier, if they had not objected to taking advice as much as they did salts and senna.

"Very well, Amy, if your heart is set upon it, and you see your way through without too great an outlay of money, time, and temper, I'll say no more. Talk it over with the girls, and whichever way you decide, I'll do my best to help you."

Writing a Response to Literature Prompt

Based on the author's description of Amy's character, why do you think Mrs. March concludes that experience is an "excellent teacher"? Predict what will happen when Amy has her party. Plan your response on the following page. Write your final response on pages 191 and 192.

Writer's Checklist

✔ **A well-written response to reading:**

☐ is formed based on an understanding of the writing prompt.

☐ contains the writer's own thoughts about the text.

☐ gives examples from the text to support opinions.

Directions: Plan your response in the space below.

Directions: Write your response on the lines below.

_____

_____

_____

_____

_____

_____

_____

_____

_____

_____

_____

_____

_____

_____

_____

_____

_____

_____

_____

CCSs: W.8.7, WHST.6-8.7

Lesson 16: Research and Technology

Sometimes you need information in a hurry. What's the difference between *anecdote* and *antidote*? How many people live in Quito, Ecuador? Which mammals lay eggs? The answers can be found in reference materials. This lesson will teach you some tips on how to collect information from various sources as you prepare to write informational reports.

As you already know, informational reports rely on facts. And most of the time you don't have all the facts you need stored away in your brain. That's where the research part comes in. If you know where to find references and how to use them, your job as a researcher will be that much easier.

Preparing to write an informational report for school (or, someday, for your employer) is a straightforward process even if your subject matter is complex.

 ## TIP 1: Pick a topic.

You might start with a topic that has been assigned to you by your teacher or brainstorm some ideas until you find one that appeals to you.

Something like "dogs" is too big a topic, unless you're writing a book. A narrower topic such as "training your dog" might still be too big if you have to write only three or four pages. Keep narrowing it down until you get to a specific topic you can cover well in the space you have been given, such as "housebreaking your dog." Don't make it too narrow, though. Your topic should provide enough content for the length of your paper.

 ## TIP 2: Ask questions to guide your search.

One useful way to decide what information you need to find is to ask yourself what you want to know about the subject. Imagine you decide to write about the dachshund breed of dogs. Some of the questions you might be interested in answering include:

> Why are they called dachshunds?
> How did they get long bodies and short legs?

Think about other questions you might like to ask. As you find the answers, you will probably think of other questions you want to know about. Let your curiosity lead you.

CCSs: W.8.7, W.8.8, WHST.6-8.7, WHST.6-8.8

 ## TIP 3: Know where to find the information you need.

The best source of information is your librarian. A good librarian is the ultimate "search engine," someone who can help you find reliable, accurate information in a flash. But after talking to the librarian, the next stop is the references themselves. The following tips list reference materials and their uses.

 ## TIP 4: Encyclopedias give general information about almost any topic.

Encyclopedias contain basic information about a subject. They are not as up-to-date as newspapers and magazines. In other words, if you want information about your favorite new rock group, you won't find anything in the encyclopedia. If you want information on the history of rock and roll, an encyclopedia might be just the thing you need.

Usually, an encyclopedia includes several volumes. Typically, publishers organize encyclopedias so that each letter of the alphabet gets its own book. However, sometimes they have to split up a letter into more than one volume. For example, an encyclopedia might have volumes labeled "Sa to Sl" and "Sm to Sz."

Entries in encyclopedias are arranged alphabetically by key words. Guide words appear at the top corner of each page and tell you the first and last term included on that page. They make it easier to find the subject you are looking for.

When you are doing research, there may be several different terms you could look for. Try to narrow the focus of your search by beginning with the most specific key word. For example, if you wanted to find information on rock music, you could look under *music*, but you might find information on a lot of different kinds of music. Instead, you could look under *rock* and find more specific information on rock music. If the word you choose to look for doesn't give you enough information, broaden your focus a little at a time.

1. The man known as the "president of the Underground Railroad," Levi Coffin, was an abolitionist leader who helped more than 2,000 slaves escape to freedom.

   Which phrase would be most helpful in finding more information about this famous abolitionist leader's life?

   A. abolitionist leaders

   B. Underground Railroad

   C. Levi Coffin

   D. escape to freedom

CCSs: W.8.7, W.8.8, WHST.6-8.7, WHST.6-8.8

Using an Index

The most reliable method of finding information in most reference works is to use the index. An **index** lists every subject covered in the entire encyclopedia—alphabetically, of course.

An encyclopedia index entry for *rock* may look something like this:

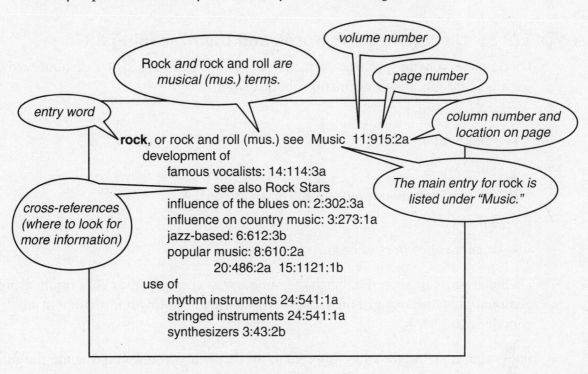

Use the index to answer Numbers 2 through 4.

2. Where will you most likely find information on the use of guitars in rock music?

   volume _____   page _____   column _____

3. Which volume and page tell where to find out about rock's effect on country music?

   A. 2:302

   B. 3:273

   C. 6:612

   D. 15:1121

4. Which of these topics is most likely discussed in volume 3 on page 43?

   A. the types of guitars used in rock music

   B. the connection between rock and jazz

   C. the names of popular rock and roll singers

   D. the use of computer synthesizers in rock music

 TIP 5: Dictionaries list words and their meanings.

Dictionaries contain specific information about words. You can use a dictionary to find out any of the following information about a word:

- correct spelling

- pronunciation

- syllables

- part of speech (noun, verb, adjective, and so on)

- definition

- language or country of origin

Dictionaries are organized in much the same way as encyclopedias. As a result, using a dictionary requires many of the same skills you use for finding information in an encyclopedia.

For example, to find the entry for *pizza* in the dictionary, you would first use the guide words to find the right page. The next step would be to scan the page until you came to the entry word you're looking for.

> **piz•za** (pēt′sə), a spicy Italian dish made by baking a large flat layer of bread dough covered with cheese, tomato sauce, herbs, etc. *n.*, *pl.* **piz•zas**.
>
> – from the *Scott Foresman Intermediate Dictionary*, copyright © 1979

The entry word is followed by a pronunciation and a definition. An abbreviation within the entry also tells the word's part of speech.

CCSs: W.8.7, W.8.8, WHST.6-8.7, WHST.6-8.8

 TIP 6: Almanacs contain lists of facts.

Like an encyclopedia, an **almanac** contains information about a wide variety of subjects. Unlike most encyclopedias, this reference book is updated and reprinted every year. So, what else distinguishes an almanac from an encyclopedia? It may be most helpful to look at some examples of what both references contain.

Examples of Things You Might Look for in a Current ...

Almanac	Encyclopedia
the number of satellites launched during the past year	a description of the movements of the planets around the sun
a list of the year's Nobel Prize winners	a general history of the Nobel Prize
win-loss records of every National Football League team for the past season	a general overview of the history of professional football teams
population statistics for every county in your state	a broad range of information about the states
heights of the world's tallest buildings	the history of skyscrapers in the United States
a list of major exports of each country in Europe	an explanation of the European free-market system
maps showing last year's boundary changes	maps with boundaries from the year of publication

When in doubt, remember that an almanac usually contains lists, current statistics, and specific detailed information. An encyclopedia usually contains historical overviews and general information, along with some specifics.

5. Which information would most likely be found in a world almanac?

    A. a biography of inventor Thomas Alva Edison

    B. Zimbabwe's gross domestic product last year

    C. an explanation of the causes of the Russian Revolution of 1917

    D. a discussion of the economic impact of the Panama Canal being opened

6. Which heading is least likely to be found in a world almanac?

    A. Directory of International Labor Unions

    B. Principal Languages of the Modern World

    C. Human Nervous System, Structure and Function

    D. Immigration into the United States by Country of Last Residence

197

TIP 7: Atlases contain maps.

An **atlas** is a book of maps. Various kinds of atlases serve different purposes. For example, if you want to plan a car trip across the United States, a road atlas will be a helpful tool. To locate a foreign city you've heard about in the news, an international atlas is a good resource. To plan a backpacking trip into the Rockies, an atlas showing geographical features of that area would be the logical choice.

An atlas is more than just maps, though. Atlases may also contain:

- latitude and longitude coordinates
- topography (types of land)
- population figures
- elevations
- settlement patterns
- agricultural patterns
- transportation routes

It is important to know when to use an atlas. Keep in mind the features of the various references as you answer the following questions.

7. An atlas would be the best choice of references for which of these tasks?

    A. listing the main products of the coastal plain

    B. writing a report about the United States government

    C. learning about the formation of the Grand Canyon

    D. planning a car trip from Denver, Colorado, to Chicago, Illinois

8. Which of these would least likely be part of an international atlas?

    A. the location of the Everglades

    B. the elevation of Alaska's Mt. McKinley

    C. the history of the Egyptian pyramids

    D. the population of Munich, Germany

CCSs: W.8.7, W.8.8, WHST.6-8.7, WHST.6-8.8

 TIP 8: Use periodicals to find information and opinions about current events.

Newspapers, magazines, and journals are called **periodicals** because they are printed periodically, on a regularly scheduled basis.

Newspapers are usually printed daily, but some may be issued weekly. They contain very current news articles, interesting feature stories on topics of local or widespread interest, editorials that tell the editors' opinions about a topic, and letters to the editor written by community members who have something they want to say to the newspaper editor or the public.

Newspapers carry advertisements designed to sell products. They also contain public information such as announcements of recent births, engagements, weddings, anniversaries, and obituaries; police bulletins telling who was arrested for what type of crime; and government notices, such as city council proceedings or other civic business.

You can expect news articles, public service information, and feature stories to be factual. You can count on editorials and letters to the editor to state opinions. And you can be assured that advertisements will do their best to persuade, even if only by the attractive way in which the product is displayed.

Magazines are usually printed either weekly or monthly, though some are issued less frequently. Magazines almost always focus on a particular topic, such as auto racing, celebrities, sports, or current events. If you read an article from *People*, what do you expect it to be about? Most likely it will tell about a public figure who is in the news or a lesser-known person who has done something remarkable.

Magazines are published less often than newspapers. Major stories are usually covered in greater depth in a magazine than in a newspaper. Like newspapers, magazines often contain news articles, feature stories, editorials, letters to the editor, and advertising.

An even more narrowly focused type of magazine is called a professional **journal**. This type of periodical is targeted to a particular group of professionals. You can usually tell who the target audience is by looking carefully at the title. For example, you may have heard of the *Journal of the American Medical Association*, which is written for physicians.

9. Which of the following magazines would be the best source of information on the latest designs in miniature radio-controlled cars?

    A. *Automotive Quarterly*

    B. *Car Modeler*

    C. *Car and Driver*

    D. *Radio-Controlled Model Airplane News*

 TIP 9: The Internet is a vast source of information—and misinformation.

The **Internet** is a global computer network. You can find information on almost any subject by searching the World Wide Web, the part of the Internet that is designed for easy navigation. Because there's so much material on the Web, you need a strategy for finding what you want. Before you start, check with your librarian for information on how to search effectively.

You must also carefully evaluate the information you find. Just because it's on the Web doesn't mean it's fair, unbiased, or accurate. One good way to determine whether a Web site is offering unbiased information is to decide whether the Web site is designed to sell you a product. Commercial Web sites (generally those ending in *.com*) may serve more as advertisements than as information sources. Web sites ending in *.edu*, *.org*, or *.gov* are usually more reliable. Your librarian can give you more tips on evaluating a particular Web site.

10. Which of these Web sites would most likely contain reliable information about the Old West?

    A. www.oldwest-themovie.com/about/lifeinthewest.html

    B. www.example.net/users/billjohnson/bills_old_west_pages

    C. www.egbert.university.edu/depts/history/oldwest.htm

    D. www.books4sale2u.com/subjects/oldwest.html

More Electronic Information Sources

CD-ROMs are discs containing information that can be read by a computer. Encyclopedias and dictionaries can be purchased on CD-ROM.

An **electronic database** is a collection of information organized in such a way that you can easily find the data you need. Many schools use databases to store and retrieve information about students, such as their full names, ages, parents' names, addresses, and phone numbers.

CCSs: W.8.6, W.8.7, W.8.8, WHST.6-8.6, WHST.6-8.7, WHST.6-8.8

TIP 10: Use library catalogs to find sources on a topic.

The materials in a library—books, videotapes, music CDs, and so on—are listed in a catalog so that people can easily find them. This catalog comes in one of two forms: a computer database or a collection of paper cards. It includes important information about the materials, such as the author, the location of the item, and notes about content.

Most important, the library **catalog** tells where to find material contained in the library. Every item has its own call number—a label made up of a series of numbers and letters. In most U.S. libraries, the numbering system used is the Dewey Decimal System.

It isn't necessary to learn the whole system (unless you plan to study library science), but it is important to learn how to use the system in your own library. Most libraries post signs to tell readers where to look for call numbers on the shelves. Once you know the call number of the item you need, just follow the signs to find that location in the library.

TIP 11: Use text features in resources to help you find the information you need.

There are many special text features authors can use to help readers understand a passage. Unit titles, chapter titles, headings, and subheadings serve two purposes: They tell readers what to expect, and they help organize information.

Also look for words that are underlined, boldfaced, italicized, indented, or even in colored type. These words usually provide special information.

Pay attention to any art in a passage, such as illustrations, charts, or graphs. Often, a piece of art or caption will convey information not written about in the passage.

Many reference materials include glossaries. A **glossary** is a list of the difficult words used in the text and the definitions for those words. You can skim a glossary to find out what kinds of topics the book covers.

Finally, also make sure to read any sidebars carefully. Just because sidebars are not part of the body of a text doesn't mean that they aren't worth reading. Sidebars can contribute a lot to your understanding of a piece of writing.

TIP 12: Gather information.

Go to the library, open an encyclopedia, get on the Internet, read a book or a magazine article, interview an expert . . . The ways to gather information are limited only by your imagination.

You will probably want to make notes as you gather information, whether it's from a book or a real person. You can keep your notes on cards, in a notebook, or in a computer document. Here are a few tips for note-taking:

- Write down the most important ideas and supporting details.

- Make clear whether you are quoting the source directly, summarizing, or paraphrasing. **Summarizing** means writing a brief statement of the major ideas and details. **Paraphrasing** means putting specific ideas from the source into your own words.

- Accurately record where you found each piece of information in the source, such as the chapter and page number.

- Create a system that will help you sort your notes later. This could be based on the research questions you are asking.

- When taking notes during interviews, follow the tips above. Also, ask questions if you don't understand something. Ask for the spellings of names. Review your notes just after the interview to make sure you've had all your questions answered. If you plan to use a tape recorder, ask for permission first.

 TIP 13: Determine the credibility of your sources.

It's one thing to find information on a topic. It's another to find accurate information on a topic. Just because something appears in print or on a computer screen doesn't make it true. How can you tell whether a source is credible, or believable?

There are a few general questions you should think about when evaluating a source: What is the quality of the information? Is there reason to believe the information is credible and accurate? Is this information useful?

CCSs: W.8.8, W.8.9, WHST.6-8.8

Use these guidelines to help you determine the validity of your sources:

Quality

- Where was the information published? (For example, does the article appear in a tabloid newspaper or in a respected professional journal?)

- Is the information objective? (Is the information based on fact or opinion? What are the author's purpose and bias?)

Authority and Accuracy

- What is the author's background? (What makes him or her an "expert"? What is the author's field of expertise?)

- What are the author's sources? (Is a bibliography included? What is the basis of the article?)

- What is the reputation of the author? (Is the author linked to a recognizable and credible institution? What kind of training has he or she received?)

Usefulness

- Is the source current? (What is the publication date? Is the Web site kept up-to-date?)

- Are there links to other useful sources? (Remember, when you follow a link to another Web site, you must evaluate that site's accuracy, as well.)

- What kind of coverage does the author give the topic? Does the author give a general overview or provide specific details and in-depth information?

 TIP 14: Give credit where credit is due.

Using the Web and other library resources, we can find the answer to almost any question we ask. Not only that, but all this information seems to be "free."

It may be free, but it is not ours. Authors work hard to research their information, write about it, and publish it. If you borrow an author's words or ideas without giving him or her credit, you are stealing that author's work. The technical term for stealing an author's work is **plagiarism**.

Fortunately, we can give credit to the author by citing our sources. There are rules that govern how the information should be cited. One good way to figure out the rules is to imitate existing citations. Here are some examples.

Type of Text	Example Citation
book	Huck, Eugene. *The Wonderful World of Dolphins*. New York: Pundit Publishing, 2005.
magazine article	Finn, Philippa. "Dolphins: They're Smarter Than You Think." *Aqua Life*. August 2008: 20–22.
encyclopedia article	"Dolphin." *World Book Encyclopedia*. 2006.
Web site	"AquaFacts: Dolphins and Porpoises." *OceanLink*. 21 Sept. 2008. Vancouver Aquarium Marine Science Centre. 28 Mar. 2009. http://oceanlink.island.net/aquafacts/dolphin.html.

11. Choose a book, a magazine article, an encyclopedia article, or a Web site from your classroom or library resources, and write a citation for your selection on the following lines.

_____

_____

_____

After you have finished your research, you will create a works-cited list or a bibliography at the end of your writing. A **works-cited** list is a list of the sources you have specifically mentioned in your paper. A **bibliography** is a list of all the sources you have used, whether or not you have cited them.

Using Quotations

A quotation should never stand alone as an entire sentence. Introduce the quote with a complete sentence followed by a colon, use an introductory phrase and a comma, or make the quote part of your own sentence. Here are some examples.

• Mark Twain issued a characteristic tongue-in-cheek warning: "Be careful about reading health books. You may die of a misprint."

• According to Eleanor Roosevelt, "It is not fair to ask of others what you are unwilling to do yourself."

• Although Helen Keller believed "the world is full of suffering," she felt "it is full also of the overcoming of it."

CCSs: W.8.8, WHST.6-8.8

When you use quotations or information from one of your sources in your text, let readers know by using in-text citations (sometimes called parenthetical notations) or endnotes.

Use **in-text citations** to reference sources within the text of your report. In-text citations direct readers to full citations in the works-cited list or bibliography. Note the author's last name and relevant page number in parentheses at the end of your sentence. Here is an example.

> Dolphins are highly intelligent animals capable of learning language and behaviors, even how to use tools. Dolphins off the coast of Australia carry sponges on the end of their beaks to protect them from spiny urchins as they forage for food on the seafloor (Finn 21).

An **endnote** is a numbered note that appears at the end of the text. It can explain an idea or give the source for a quotation or paraphrased information. Endnotes are indicated in the text by a superscript number (a number printed above the line). Look at the example below.

1. Eugene Huck. *The Wonderful World of Dolphins* (New York: Pundit Publishing, 2005), p. 180.

Your teacher will give you more instructions about how he or she wants you to cite your sources. Remember, record all of the details about your sources so you can cite them properly!

Lesson Practice begins on the following page.

Directions: This passage is about Frederick Douglass. Read the passage. Then answer Numbers 1 and 2.

The slave narrative is a particular branch of nonfiction that recounts the experiences of African Americans who lived as slaves. One of the most famous slave narratives was written by a man named Frederick Douglass.

Frederick Douglass was born into slavery in 1818. As a young boy, he lived as a houseboy (a slave who worked in the house) for the Auld family in Baltimore, Maryland. Sophia Auld taught him the alphabet, but her husband forbade her from teaching him anything else. It was actually illegal to teach slaves to read, so Douglass taught himself. He kept schoolbooks in secret and gave away his food to neighborhood boys in exchange for reading and writing lessons.

Douglass grew into one of the most famous abolitionists in history. He eventually published his own newspaper, wrote three autobiographies, and became an advisor to Abraham Lincoln.

adapted from

A Narrative on the Life of Frederick Douglass, an American Slave

by Frederick Douglass

I lived in Master Hugh's family about seven years. During this time, I succeeded in learning to read and write. In accomplishing this, I was compelled to resort to various stratagems. I had no regular teacher. My mistress, who had kindly commenced to instruct me, had, in compliance with the advice and direction of her husband, not only ceased to instruct, but had set her face against my being instructed by any one. It is due, however, to my mistress to say of her, that she did not adopt this course of treatment immediately. She at first lacked the depravity indispensable to shutting me up in mental darkness. It was at least necessary for her to have some training in the exercise of irresponsible power, to make her equal to the task of treating me as though I were a brute.

My mistress was, as I have said, a kind and tender-hearted woman; and in the simplicity of her soul she commenced, when I first went to live with her, to treat me as she supposed one human being ought to treat another. In entering upon the duties of a slaveholder, she did not seem to perceive that I sustained to her the relation of a mere chattel, and that for her to treat me as a human being was not only wrong, but dangerously so. Slavery proved as injurious to her as it did to me. When I went there, she was a pious, warm, and tender-hearted woman. There was no sorrow or suffering for which she had not a tear. She had bread for the hungry, clothes for the naked, and comfort for every mourner that came within her reach. Slavery soon proved its ability to divest her of these heavenly qualities. Under its influence, the tender heart became stone, and the lamblike disposition gave way to one of tiger-like fierceness.

The first step in her downward course was in her ceasing to instruct me. She now commenced to practice her husband's precepts. She finally became even more violent in her opposition than her husband himself. She was not satisfied with simply doing as well as he had commanded; she seemed anxious to do better. Nothing seemed to make her more angry than to see me with a newspaper. She seemed to think that here lay the danger. I have had her rush at me with a face made all up of fury, and snatch from me a newspaper, in a manner that fully revealed her apprehension. She was an apt woman; and a little experience soon demonstrated, to her satisfaction, that education and slavery were incompatible with each other.

From this time I was most narrowly watched. If I was in a separate room any considerable length of time, I was sure to be suspected of having a book, and was at once called to give an account of myself. All this, however, was too late. The first step had been taken. Mistress, in teaching me the alphabet, had given me the inch, and no precaution could prevent me from taking the ell.

The plan which I adopted, and the one by which I was most successful, was that of making friends of all the little white boys whom I met in the street. As many of these as I could, I converted into teachers. With their kindly aid, obtained at different times and in different places, I finally succeeded in learning to read. When I was sent of errands, I always took my book with me, and by going one part of my errand quickly, I found time to get a lesson before my return. I used also to carry bread with me, enough of which was always in the house, and to which I was always welcome; for I was much better off in this regard than many of the poor white children in our neighborhood. This bread I used to bestow upon the hungry little urchins, who, in return, would give me that more valuable bread of knowledge. I am strongly tempted to give the names of two or three of those little boys, as a testimonial of the gratitude and affection I bear them; but prudence forbids;—not that it would injure me, but it might embarrass them; for it is almost an unpardonable offence to teach slaves to read in this Christian country. It is enough to say of the dear little fellows, that they lived on Philpot Street, very near Durgin and Bailey's ship-yard. I used to talk this matter of slavery over with them. I would sometimes say to them, I wished I could be as free as they would be when they got to be men. "You will be free as soon as you are twenty-one, but I am a slave for life! Have not I as good a right to be free as you have?" These words used to trouble them; they would express for me the liveliest sympathy, and console me with the hope that something would occur by which I might be free.

1.   Select a topic to research based on what you have read. It should be something more specific than "slavery" or "Frederick Douglass." Write your topic on the line below.

_____

_____

2.   Identify three sources you would need to conduct your research and what kind of information you would be looking for with each source.

Source 1: _____

_____

_____

_____

_____

_____

_____

Source 2: _____

_____

_____

_____

_____

_____

_____

Source 3: _____

_____

_____

_____

_____

_____

_____

UNIT 3

Language

You've gathered your ideas and organized them; you've cast them into perfect words, elegant sentences, and well-ordered paragraphs. You have finished your masterpiece—or have you? If you want to be certain that your reader will enjoy your best work, you still have some work to do.

The next part of the writing process is revising and editing your work. Now is the time to read carefully what you have written, sentence by sentence, word by word. You want to check the presentation of your ideas as well as the technical details of your writing. This unit will show you how to turn your rough draft into a good, solid (and, perhaps, fabulous) piece of writing.

In This Unit

Verbs

Punctuation

Spelling

CCSs: L.8.1b, L.8.1c, L.8.3a

Lesson 17: Verbs

Verbs provide the action in your writing. Choosing the right verbs can make your writing practically jump off the page. On the other hand, few things are more distracting for a reader than mistakes in verb usage. In this lesson, you'll review the skills that will help you avoid the most common verb-related errors.

TIP 1: There are three primary verb tenses: past, present, and future.

> Yesterday, we will be going to the movies, but there is a snowstorm, so we went tomorrow before we would get caught in the blizzard.

You would probably never write a sentence with as many mistakes in it as the one above, but verb-tense problems are common for most writers. You need to understand verb tense so that you can tell your reader when things happen.

TIP 2: Use past–tense verbs for events that happened in the past.

Look at these sentences that correctly use past-tense verbs.

> When I was in kindergarten, I <u>ate</u> crayons.
> Yesterday, I <u>went</u> to the mall with my friends.

1. Write your own sentence using a past-tense verb.

_____

_____

CCSs: L.8.1b, L.8.1c, L.8.3a

 TIP 3: **Use present-tense verbs for events that are happening now.**

Here are two sentences that correctly use present-tense verbs.

> Now that I am in eighth grade, I <u>eat</u> massive quantities of nachos.
> Right now, I <u>am</u> going to the mall with my friends.

2. Write your own sentence using a present-tense verb.

_____

_____

 TIP 4: **Use future-tense verbs for events that will happen in the future.**

Look at the following sentences that correctly use future-tense verbs.

> When I am in high school, I <u>will join</u> the basketball team.
> When I am older, I <u>will drive</u> to the mall with my friends.

3. Write your own sentence using a future-tense verb.

_____

_____

 TIP 5: **Verbals are verb forms used as nouns, adjectives, or adverbs.**

A **verbal** is a word formed from a verb but used as a noun or modifier. There are three kinds of verbals: gerunds, participles, and infinitives.

A **gerund** ends in *-ing* and functions as a noun.

> <u>Swimming</u> is a great way to burn calories.
> Cassie tried to ignore her brother's <u>whining</u>.

A **participle** is a verbal that functions as an adjective. Present participles end in -*ing*, and past participles usually end in -*ed* but may also end in -*en*, -*d*, -*t*, or -*n*.

> <u>Glowing</u> fireflies filled the sky. (functions as a modifier of *fireflies*)
> The pirates searched for <u>hidden</u> treasures.
> (functions as a modifier of *treasures*)

An **infinitive** consists of the word *to* plus a verb in its stem form (*walk, run, jump, fly,* and so on). Infinitives can function as nouns, adjectives, or adverbs.

> <u>To apologize</u> is the best course of action.
> (functions as both a noun and subject)
> Ellie has a speech <u>to prepare</u>. (functions as an adjective modifying *speech*)
> We must practice <u>to improve</u>. (functions as an adverb modifying *practice*)

Because verbals look like verbs, some writers make the mistake of using them in place of verbs. Notice how they are used in the chart below. Then write your own corrections for Numbers 4 and 5.

Incorrect	Correct
Flying, his greatest fear.	Flying was his greatest fear.
The soaring bird across the sky.	The bird soared across the sky.
To win, their only ambition.	4.
Dust is Olivia's most dreaded chore.	5.

TIP 6: Know the difference between active voice and passive voice.

When you write in the **active voice**, the subject of a sentence performs the action of the verb. *I ate the pizza.* In this sentence, *I* is the subject and *I* performs the action of the verb: *I ate.*

In the **passive voice**, the subject of a sentence is acted upon. *The pizza was eaten by me.* In this sentence, *pizza* is the subject, and it is acted upon: *The pizza was eaten.*

Sentences using the passive voice will always have a verb containing some form of *be—am*, *is*, *was*, *were*, *are*, or *been*. Look at these examples.

Active: Norman started the fire when he tried to grill a hot dog for his little sister.

Passive: The fire was started by Norman trying to grill a hot dog for his little sister.

See the difference? Active verbs communicate powerfully and directly, and your writing will generally have more force if you stick to the active voice.

Rewrite these sentences using the active voice.

6. Saria's shirt was accidentally ripped by me.

   _____

7. The ship was pulled into the harbor by the tugboat.

   _____

While it's a good idea to strive for an active voice in most of your writing, there are times when the passive voice might actually suit you better. Maybe you want to show a character's uncertainty or passive nature. In this case, using the passive voice can help your readers get into the minds of your characters.

> When they broke up, Ben fell into a deep funk. He couldn't get out of bed to eat or bathe, and he refused to talk to any of his friends. His phone went unanswered. His computer screen remained dark.

The last two sentences are in the passive voice, and illustrate Ben's state of mind. The writer could have said, "He didn't answer his phone. He didn't turn on his computer," but the passive voice allows readers to really experience Ben's state of mind.

TIP 7: Know your verb moods.

Verb **mood** is different from tense and voice, but these all go hand in hand. Verb moods convey the speaker's intent. The following paragraphs list the common moods. The mood you choose will depend on what kind of writing you're doing.

The **indicative** mood is used for declarative sentences. Writers use the indicative mood to state facts or opinions. Most of the sentences you write will be in this mood.

> Jason <u>ran</u> to the grocery store.
> Mrs. McAllister's new kitchen <u>is</u> the envy of the neighborhood.

8. Write a sentence using the indicative mood.

_____

The **interrogative** mood is used when asking a question.

> <u>Will</u> you please <u>call</u> me when you arrive?
> <u>Do</u> you <u>think</u> this sweater is too expensive?

9. Write a sentence using the interrogative mood.

_____

CCSs: L.8.1c, L.8.3a

The **imperative** mood is used to give a command. Since the subject "you" is understood, verbs in the imperative mood are always in the second-person.

> <u>Get</u> down from there.
> <u>Meet</u> me in the hallway outside biology as soon as class is over.

10. Write a sentence using the imperative mood.

_____

Indicative, interrogative, and imperative moods are used most often with simple, straightforward sentences. As sentences and ideas get more complex, you may have to choose a more complex verb mood, such as subjunctive or conditional.

The **subjunctive** mood is only used in special circumstances, most often to express a wish or to illustrate a hypothetical situation. The subjunctive mood can be tricky, so there are a few rules to familiarize yourself with. Once you're comfortable with the subjunctive mood, you'll be able to hear the correct verb tense to use.

Here are some examples:

- When using writing in the present tense, use the past tense of a subjunctive verb.

  I wish I <u>had</u> a red hat to match my shoes.

- When *to be* is the verb in a subjunctive sentence, always use *were*.

  If I <u>were</u> there, you'd be having more fun.

A good rule of thumb to follow is that sentences in the subjunctive mood often begin with *If*.

11. Write a sentence using the subjunctive mood.

_____

The **conditional** mood is often linked with the subjunctive, as it can also be used for hypothetical situations. Conditional clauses are set off with words like *might*, *could*, and *would*, and indicate an event that will cause something else to happen.

> If we <u>go</u> to Paris this summer, I <u>might try</u> escargot.
> If we <u>had jumped</u> off that bridge, we <u>would have</u> broken our legs.

12. Write a sentence using the conditional mood.

_____

 TIP 8: Recognize shifts in tense and mood.

It is important to maintain consistency in your writing. In Lesson 11 you learned about point of view, and how switching points of view can be confusing for your readers. The same is true of verb tenses and mood. Be aware of shifts in tense and mood to make your writing as clear as possible.

Lesson Practice begins on the following page.

Directions: Answer Numbers 1 through 5.

1. **Read this sentence.**

    Yesterday June and Alex <u>have fought</u> about whose turn it was to do the dishes.

    Which of the following should replace the underlined verb phrase?

    A. are fighting

    B. fought

    C. to fight

    D. will fight

2. **Read this sentence.**

    If Jose doesn't pull up his French grade, he <u>stays</u> behind in summer school.

    Which of the following should replace the underlined verb?

    A. will stay

    B. has stayed

    C. stayed

    D. is staying

3. **Read this sentence.**

    Jess and Lory have decided to enter the battle of the bands contest.

    Which verb mood is used in this sentence?

    A. imperative

    B. interrogative

    C. indicative

    D. subjunctive

4. **Read this sentence.**

    If my sister was a character in a fairy tale, she'll be the evil queen.

    Rewrite this sentence using the correct verb tense and mood. Then identify which mood you used.

    _____

    _____

    _____

    _____

5. **Read this sentence.**

    In a few short years, Evie rises through the ranks of the company from mail clerk to vice president.

    Rewrite this sentence using the correct verb tense and mood. Then identify which mood you used.

    _____

    _____

    _____

    _____

CCSs: L.8.2a, L.8.2b

Lesson 18: Punctuation

There, are so many! punctuation rules. I mean; how? am I ever going to, remember: them all. And 'why does it really matter anyway.' Before you know it! the grammar police, will be knocking on my door. "wondering, what youre going to do, a'bout that comma you misplaced"?

There might seem to be more punctuation rules than one person can ever remember. However, a few basic guidelines will help you through most situations. You will have an opportunity to review those guidelines in this lesson.

Remember, your main goal as a writer is to communicate your ideas to your readers. Using correct punctuation will help you make your meaning clear.

End Punctuation

Deciding how to end a sentence is the easiest part of punctuation. You have only three choices: the question mark, the exclamation point, and the period.

 TIP 1: **Use a question mark (?) for sentences that ask a question.**

Is that your raccoon on top of the refrigerator?

 TIP 2: **Save the exclamation point (!) for statements made with a great deal of emotion or excitement.**

Get that chipmunk out of your sock drawer!

 TIP 3: **Use a period (.) for all other kinds of statements.**

I asked Thomas to do his impersonation of a red-bellied woodpecker.

Ellipsis

An **ellipsis** is a series of three periods with spaces between them. When used in the middle of a sentence, it shows that some information has been left out. When used at the end of a sentence, it indicates the continuation of an idea.

Commas (,)

Commas tell your readers to pause for a moment before continuing to read. They also help separate words or phrases that shouldn't be blended into the rest of the sentence. There are many situations in which commas should be used, but many of them are covered by the following tips.

 TIP 4: Use commas after items in a series.

If three or more items are listed in a row, place a comma after each item in the series except the last one.

> She brought a sandwich, a juice box, and a bag of baby carrots for lunch.
> Last night I finished my homework, watched some TV, and practiced playing the accordion.

 TIP 5: Use a comma after an introductory phrase.

An **introductory phrase** is a phrase that introduces the main idea of a sentence. It appears at the beginning of the sentence and is followed by a comma.

> Every evening around eight, I take my dog for a walk.
> By the end of the race, I was exhausted.
> Built for speed, the motorless go-cart isn't very comfortable for passengers.

 TIP 6: Use a comma after a subordinate introductory clause.

A **subordinate clause** is a phrase that includes both a subject and a verb but does not express a complete thought. When using a subordinate clause at the beginning of a sentence, you should follow it with a comma.

> Although I don't really like artichoke burgers, I ate one for lunch.
> Whatever you want to eat, you can find it at Bluto's.

CCSs: L.8.2a, L.8.2b

 TIP 7: **Use commas to set off descriptive phrases or appositives.**

An **appositive** is a word or phrase that describes a noun or a pronoun. Appositives are set off by commas.

> That man, the one with the parrot on his shoulder, says he used to be a pirate.
> I am reading a new book by Edgar Graves, the noted horror writer.

 TIP 8: **Use commas to set off phrases or expressions that interrupt the sentence.**

A **parenthetical expression** is a side remark and is not needed for understanding the main idea of the sentence. Parenthetical expressions are set off by commas.

Some common parenthetical expressions are *as a matter of fact*, *believe me*, and *if you ask me*.

> Creampuff is, without a doubt, the meanest hamster alive.
> My favorite food, believe it or not, is liver-and-cabbage salad.

Dash

Another way to punctuate an interruption in a sentence is to use a pair of **dashes**. A dash represents a stronger pause than a comma.

 TIP 9: **Use a comma in direct address.**

A **direct address** is the noun used when you are speaking directly to someone. Direct addresses are set off by commas.

> Dad, can I borrow your skateboard?
> Hey, P.J., where are you going?
> Tomorrow, class, we will be taking a test.

 TIP 10: **Use commas in dialogue.**

> "I really need to get inside," Tasmin moaned, "before I melt."

TIP 11: Use commas after both the greetings and closings of letters.

Dear Jamal,

Sincerely,

This is just a partial list of the many uses of commas. Commas are also used for dates, addresses, and a variety of other purposes.

Semicolons (;)

 TIP 12: Use semicolons to connect two or more closely related thoughts in a single sentence.

A semicolon can only go between two clauses that could be complete sentences by themselves. Do not use a semicolon to connect clauses if there is a conjunction (*and, but, or, nor, for, so*) between them; use a comma before the conjunction instead.

Incorrect: Trudy swam the entire length of the pool underwater; and you should have seen her face when she came up for air.

Correct: Trudy swam the entire length of the pool underwater; you should have seen her face when she came up for air.

Correct: Trudy swam the entire length of the pool underwater, and you should have seen her face when she came up for air.

Correct: Trudy swam the entire length of the pool underwater. You should have seen her face when she came up for air.

Colons (:)

 TIP 13: Use a colon to punctuate business letter salutations.

Business letters are more formal than friendly letters. The salutation, or greeting, in a business letter should be followed by a colon.

Dear Sir: Dear Mrs. Edwards:

Lesson Practice begins on the following page.

Directions: Imagine that you're the editor of your school paper. A student has just given you a copy of a story about students' summer plans, but it is missing some punctuation. Read the passage, adding the proper punctuation marks where they are needed.

What to Do This Summer

by Omar Walters

It's almost the end of the year and students' thoughts are turning away from books and toward their summer plans While some students enjoy the thought of three months free to play video games in their basements others are looking forward to a summer of real action

"I'm looking forward to basketball camp which I've been going to since I was little," says Renee Hutchinson who is a starting forward on the girls basketball team. Hutchinson describes a day in the life of a basketball camper. "It's really hard We do three or four hours of drills in the morning. In the afternoon we focus on improving our all-around game We usually play a couple of scrimmage games Then its time for dinner. At the end of a long day like that you just want to eat a pizza and go to sleep"

It might be hard work but its kept Hutchinson at the top of her game

While some students will be building their muscles others will be filling their piggy banks over the summer Casper Johnson says he is looking forward to the money he'll earn from his usual summer job detasseling corn

"It's hard work, but the pay is really good" says Johnson. This will be his second season detasseling corn. "Last summer, I didn't know what I was doing. I didn't wear gloves and my hands got all cut up. That corn can be sharp This year, I'll be prepared"

Despite killer corn and the summer heat, quite a few students detassel over the summer because its one of the few jobs open to them

You have to be 14 or even 16 to work most jobs in town, says Nathan Hauke a student who also detassels. "But to detassel you only have to be 12 or 13 and the money is really good. I like to go out with my friends on the weekends and it's good to have some cash to see movies and eat out once in awhile

Lesson 19: Spelling

Are you good at spelling? Some people seem to have a natural gift for it. But, if you're not a great speller, it's not too late to become one. Read more books. Learn the basic spelling rules. Look up words you're not sure about. As with any activity, the more you practice, the better you'll get.

One of the easiest ways to become a better speller is to understand how affixes change the spelling of root words. You learned about roots and affixes in Lesson 1. For each of the rules listed in this lesson, complete the chart by writing the correct spelling of the affixed word.

 TIP 1: Do not change the root word when adding a suffix that begins with a consonant, unless the root word ends in *y*.

Root	Suffix	Affixed Word
clear	-ly	clearly
eager	-ness	eagerness
care	-less	1.

 TIP 2: In general, if a root word ends in a *y*, change the *y* to an *i* before adding a suffix.

Root	Suffix	Affixed Word
study	-ous	studious
silly	-ness	silliness
glory	-fy	2.

CCS: L.8.2c

If the suffix begins with an *i*, however, do not change the *y*.

Root	Suffix	Affixed Word
try	-ing	trying
play	-ing	3.

 TIP 3: **If the root word ends in a silent *e* and the suffix begins with a vowel, drop the silent *e*.**

Root	Suffix	Affixed Word
shine	-ing	shining
desire	-able	desirable
dance	-er	dancer
grease	-y	4.
remove	-al	5.

 TIP 4: **If the root word ends in *e* and the suffix begins with a consonant, keep the silent *e*.**

Root	Suffix	Affixed Word
move	-ment	movement
hope	-ful	hopeful
grace	-ful	6.

The words *truly* and *wholly* are exceptions to this rule.

TIP 5: Sometimes you will have to double the final consonant of the root word.

Use this rule for:

- words ending in a consonant with only one vowel in front of it

Root	Suffix	Affixed Word
patrol	-ing	patrolling
forgot	-ten	forgotten
recap	-ing	7.

- words with only one syllable

Root	Suffix	Affixed Word
clap	-ing	clapping
win	-er	winner
thin	-er	8.

- words with the accent on the last syllable

Root	Suffix	Affixed Word
refer	-al	referral
admit	-ance	admittance
permit	-ed	9.

Exceptions include *remembering* and *greedy*.

CCS: L.8.2c

Other Useful Spelling Rules

In addition to the rules about affixed words, there are some other helpful tips that can improve your spelling.

 TIP 6: **For most nouns, form the plural by simply adding *s*.**

airplane + s = airplanes
elephant + s = elephants

 TIP 7: **For words ending in *s, ss, ch, sh,* or *x*, add *es*.**

gas + es = gases
glass + es = glasses
crutch + es = crutches
bush + es = bushes
box + es = boxes

 TIP 8: **For words ending in a consonant plus *y*, change the *y* to *i* and add *es*.**

puppy + es = puppies
party + es = parties

 TIP 9: **Remember the "*i* before *e*" rule: *i* before *e* except after *c* or when saying "ay" as in *neighbor* and *weigh*.**

belief	deceit	sleigh
siege	receive	reign

Of course, there are some exceptions, such as *their, ancient, weird,* and *seize*.

✎ Practice Activity

Directions: For Numbers 1 through 8, choose the word that completes the sentence and is spelled correctly.

1. Today, Megan turned in her _____ to be the school mascot.

   A. applecation

   B. applycation

   C. application

   D. applikation

2. Chad told his parents about the theft, _____ the fact that he had forgotten to lock up his bicycle on the day it was stolen.

   A. omiting

   B. omitting

   C. ommiting

   D. ommitting

3. Chocolate was the missing _____ in his recipe.

   A. engradient

   B. ingredient

   C. ingreedyent

   D. ingrediant

4. The jury spent 36 hours discussing the case before its members' votes were _____ .

   A. unanimus

   B. unanimuss

   C. unanimious

   D. unanimous

5. That new cereal is supposed to be _____ with iron.

   A. fortified

   B. fortifyed

   C. fourtified

   D. fourtyfied

CCS: L.8.2c

6. Chester often sat at the back of the classroom, thinking about _____.

   A. infinnity

   B. infinity

   C. infinitty

   D. infinnitty

7. All parts of the dandelion plant are _____, but not necessarily delicious.

   A. eddible

   B. edibull

   C. edible

   D. edable

8. Pam performed the experiment to prove a _____ theory.

   A. sciontific

   B. sceintific

   C. scientific

   D. sighentific

 TIP 10: Use resources to check spelling.

Whenever you come across a word that you're just not sure is spelled correctly, look it up in a dictionary. Since dictionaries list the definitions of words, you can also make sure you don't confuse a word with a similar word.

If you use a computer to write, one handy way of checking your spelling is to use the computer's spell-checking program. Spell-check scans your writing for words that are spelled incorrectly. Keep in mind, however, that these programs aren't perfect. For example, if you write the word *their* when you meant to write *they're*, the spell-checker may not recognize the mistake. There are also some kinds of words, such as proper nouns, that most spell-checkers won't recognize.

Despite all of the spelling help resources, nothing takes the place of learning spelling rules and strengthening your spelling skills.

Lesson Practice begins on the following page.

Directions: For Numbers 1 through 5, choose the phrase in which one word is spelled incorrectly.

1. A. deep channal
    B. artificial intelligence
    C. alto saxophone
    D. famous astronaut

2. A. decisive act
    B. favorite episode
    C. negative result
    D. centimental mood

3. A. high calorie
    B. security officer
    C. foreign expedittion
    D. college tuition

4. A. northern hemisphere
    B. prior obligation
    C. spooky graveyard
    D. gracefill skater

5. A. attenttive aunt
    B. gave authorization
    C. foreign diplomat
    D. identical twin

Directions: For Numbers 6 through 8, circle the misspelled word and then correctly spell the word on the line beneath the sentence.

6. Shelby was in a serious predicamant: she had forgotten her best friend's birthday.

     _____

7. Climbing Mt. Everest has to be one of the most difficult endevors of all time.

     _____

8. The lead story in every newspaper today is the trial and conviction of several corupt politicians.

     _____

UNIT 4

Speaking and Listening

Reading and writing aren't the only skills you'll need to be successful. You'll also need to work on your speaking and listening skills. Being an effective listener and speaker can be just as important as being an effective reader and writer. The same principles apply; you're just using them in a different manner. Whether you're discussing an issue in small class groups or are called on to give a persuasive speech to the entire school, there are some common tips you can use to help you convey your message clearly and confidently. The lessons in this unit will help you do just that.

In This Unit

Listening

Participating in Discussions

Speaking

235

Lesson 20: Listening

There are times when you will be called on to listen to a passage and answer questions about it rather than reading a passage in front of you. Just as there are tricks for effective reading, there are also tips for getting the most out of what you are listening to. Being a good listener involves more than just being quiet and keeping your ears open. The tips in this lesson will prepare you to be an effective listener.

 TIP 1: Take notes.

The first time you hear a passage, listen carefully but do not take notes. As the passage is read, ask yourself general questions such as the following:

- What kind of passage is it? Does it tell a fictional story? Is it a poem? Or is it a factual article about real people, places, events, or ideas?

- What is the passage mostly about? What are the main points?

If the passage gives information on a topic, keep your ears open for terms specific to that topic. If you hear a term you don't know, try to figure it out from context clues, using the skills you learned in Lesson 1.

Begin taking notes the second time you hear a passage. If the passage is fiction, note the characters, setting, and plot. Who are the main characters? What conflict do the characters face? What are the main events? How is the problem resolved?

If the passage is nonfiction, note the main idea and supporting details. What is the point the author is trying to make? Which facts help explain or argue this point?

Perhaps you're thinking, "I'll just write down everything I hear." However, if you get too caught up in writing down every word, you will miss the big picture the author is trying to get across. It is more important to understand the main idea and to remember a few important details than to jot down as much as you possibly can.

CCS: SL.8.2

Here are a few more note-taking strategies:

- Write down the most important ideas and supporting details.

- Make clear whether you are quoting the passage directly, summarizing, or paraphrasing.

- Accurately record information about the passage.

- Create a system that will help you sort your notes later. For example, imagine a passage that compares the different opinions about drilling for oil in Alaska. When you take notes, you might divide your pages into two columns: *For* on one side, recording arguments in favor of drilling, and *Against* on the other. You can choose your organizational system after you hear the passage the first time, and then use it to record your notes during the second reading.

 TIP 2: **Use notes to connect the speaker's ideas to the main idea.**

After the first reading, reflect on the passage. Remember main ideas and details, and think about how they connect. Identify your first impression and figure out what parts of the passage give you this impression.

While you wait for the passage to be read again, try to recall and organize its main points in your mind. But remember, you will hear it again—you don't have to figure everything out right now. You can get more into its details and pick up on what you may have missed when you hear it read aloud a second time.

Here are some things to think about briefly, before the passage is read again:

- Did any major themes come to mind as you listened to the passage? You learned in Lesson 2 that **themes** are universal statements the author makes about human nature and the world at large.

- How did the author use language in the passage? Was the tone formal or casual? Did the author try to impress you by using a lot of big words? Remember what you learned in Lesson 4 about literary devices and how authors use them to create mood and tone.

1. Your teacher is going to read a passage about Pocahontas. The first time your teacher reads, listen closely without taking notes. During the second reading, write down the main idea and important supporting details, using the space below.

TIP 3: Identify the speaker's purpose.

If a speaker's passage is mainly informational, you can concentrate on the main idea and the details that support that idea.

If the passage is persuasive, you'll have to do a bit more work. One of the reasons people write is to convince others that their ideas are right. Sometimes they use sound, logical arguments that hold up under inspection. Other times, authors use persuasive techniques that appeal primarily to emotions, without the foundation of a reasoned argument.

Arguments involving emotions are not always wrong. But it's important to be informed by reason when you evaluate a speaker's position. Emotions are what make issues worth arguing about, but they don't determine which side is right.

As you consider a speaker's logical shortfalls, also think about his or her possible biases. What beliefs and attitudes does the author bring to the passage? A speaker might have something to gain if others are convinced by his or her argument. Take note if the speaker suggests that anyone who disagrees with him or her is foolish. Attacking opponents, rather than their position, is a sign of bias—and of a weak argument.

TIP 4: Evaluate the speaker's message.

The author's message is connected to the main idea or theme of the passage. In an instructional passage about the dwindling population of polar bears, the speaker's message might be that we need to stop global warming or polar bears will be extinct very soon. Often, the notes you've taken while listening to the passage will allow you to connect the main idea and supporting details and come up with the speaker's message.

2. Go back to page 238 and review your notes about the Pocahontas passage. What is the speaker's message?

_____

_____

_____

_____

_____

Listening: It's Not Just For School!

Listening is a skill you need to use in class, in small group discussions, or during a test. However, the skills you learn in this lesson can also help you listen actively to friends, family, and anyone else you encounter.

• When you have conversations with friends, family, or people you've just met, listen respectfully. Use your facial expressions and body language to show your responses.

• Occasionally repeat what the other person says, in your own words. This way, people know you hear them and understand what they have to say.

• Listen carefully without judgment. Try to understand differences of opinion, and look for things you might have in common.

• Recognize when someone uses more than one level of meaning when speaking. Tune your ears to pick up figurative language and emotions when you listen. Body language can also tell you a lot.

Lesson Practice begins on the following page.

Listening

You are going to listen to a passage called "Pound Puppies." Then you will answer some questions to show how well you understood what was read.

You will listen to the passage twice. As you listen to the passage the second time, take notes.

Use the space on the next page for your notes. You may use these notes to answer the questions that follow.

As You Listen

✔ **Remember to:**

☐ focus on major ideas.

☐ identify important details.

☐ connect the speaker's ideas to the main idea.

☐ pay attention to meaning.

☐ identify the speaker's purpose.

☐ evaluate the speaker's message.

☐ take accurate notes.

Directions: Take notes in the space below.

1. What is the main idea of the passage?

   _____

   _____

   _____

2. What is the author's purpose in writing this passage?

   _____

   _____

   _____

3. Evaluate how well the author supports his argument. What kind of evidence does he offer? Do you agree or disagree with his argument?

   _____

   _____

   _____

   _____

   _____

CCS: SL.8.1a

Lesson 21: Participating in Discussions

Have you ever had a discussion with your parents or guardians about your attitude? It probably consisted mainly of them lecturing and you listening, right? What about a discussion with a younger sibling about whether or not he or she is allowed into your room? That "discussion" probably consisted of you yelling, "Stay out!" and not much else! Well, the discussions in this lesson are different. You're going to learn how to exchange ideas and engage in the give-and-take that make up a real discussion.

 TIP 1: Prepare by doing research.

You wouldn't get into a debate about football versus soccer if you didn't know the difference between a touchdown and a goal, would you? Likewise, you should not go into a class discussion without having done some research on the topic being discussed.

Imagine that your class is studying world governments. This week, you are scheduled to discuss England's monarchy. First things first: make sure you fully understand the topic. If you don't know the key terms, look them up. (A monarchy is a political system in which the head of the state is a king or a queen instead of an elected official, like a president.) Once you're clear about the topic up for discussion, you can dig deeper. For instance, you might want to research the history of England's monarchy, and the role England's current queen plays in modern society. Why does England have a queen? What does her job consist of? As you gain information, you'll start to form your own opinions based on the facts.

1. Imagine your class is going to discuss the national parks system. What might you hope to discover in your research? What resources would you use?

   _____

   _____

   _____

   _____

   _____

243

TIP 2: Work with your classmates.

Discussion entails working together. If you're working in groups, set goals and deadlines with your peers, and do your best to stick to them. Assign roles. If everyone does his or her part, the discussion will be fruitful and interesting. Working together and establishing clear goals and timelines will eliminate confusion and avoid wasting time.

If you're researching a large topic as a group such as the government of England, you might want to split up your duties. Assign a different focus to each discussion member. One person could research the history of the monarchy, another could research what the current queen does on a day-to-day basis, and so on. This way, each topic will be covered in-depth.

TIP 3: Share information with your classmates.

You can't have a discussion with just one person, right? (Perhaps you could, but it'd be pretty dull!) To discuss means "to talk about a subject with others." Class discussions are a place for you to share information and ask questions. Perhaps you've come across something in your research that you don't quite understand. Bring it up in discussion.

Ask questions about the information that your classmates have uncovered. Take notes. Evaluate one another's sources to make sure you're getting the most reliable information possible.

TIP 4: Make sure you cover a wide range of positions in your discussion.

After reading about England's monarchy, you wouldn't simply decide that the Queen is pointless because she has no real power; you'd research the other end of that opinion and discover the counterarguments. You would need to understand not only who does have the political power in England, but also whether or not the politicians look to the Queen for guidance, or if she has a say in government matters. Knowing the positions that are different from yours will allow you to argue effectively against counterarguments.

2. Some people think the national parks system should be abolished. What are some reasons for this viewpoint? Why do some people favor keeping the parks system as is?

_____

_____

_____

CCS: SL.8.1e

 TIP 5: It's okay to change your mind.

Perhaps after all of your research on England's monarchy, you have arrived at the conclusion that having a king and queen is a bit silly in this day and age, and their duties are largely ceremonial and therefore are unimportant. In the course of your discussion, new evidence is offered by one of your classmates whose parents are British. From this classmate you learn what the monarchy means to people living in Britain, which is something you didn't encounter in your own research on the duties of the monarchy.

This classmate explains that the monarchy is actually considered to be above politics. Because of this, the Queen is able to reach out to and embrace people of differing opinions and lifestyles. And because the monarchy has been in place for more than 1,000 years, the British people have come to depend on it as something stable in an ever-changing world. What's more, the Queen is viewed as an impressive ambassador to the world. As this is another angle to the issue, you must take it into consideration.

Maybe you'll change your mind about the monarchy, or maybe you won't. The important thing is that you don't dismiss the argument altogether and that you allow your views to be flexible.

Lesson Practice begins on the following page.

Directions: This passage is about the slow food movement. Read the passage. Then answer Numbers 1 through 3.

Eating Slowly

by Lauren Gilmore

You've heard of fast food, right? You probably eat it all the time. But what about slow food? It's not just eating food that takes a long time to prepare, it's a whole way of life. The slow food movement is a grassroots movement that stretches across the globe.

The slow food movement was started in 1986 by a man named Carlo Petrini. Petrini, an Italian, was upset at the prospect of a McDonald's opening in Rome. Until that time, the fast food chain hadn't had a presence in Italy, and that's the way Petrini wanted to keep things. He organized a protest, gained some followers, and this is how the slow food movement began.

Though the slow food movement is a global phenomenon, there are a few guiding principles and goals that all members share in common. First, slow food focuses on local foods, what they call "cultural cuisine." The idea is that people should eat what is grown in their area and try to preserve local food traditions. Members of the slow food movement feel that the world is losing certain traditions in the move to get everything faster and easier. We eat prepackaged foods that have been treated with all kinds of preservatives, stuff we can't even pronounce. Instead, the slow food members believe, we should look to history. What did people who lived in our areas eat before it was possible to grab a slice of pizza or a hamburger on every block?

Part of eating locally includes only eating items that are fresh and in season in your area—only eating strawberries in California from April to June, for instance. Since that is when they are grown locally, they will arrive on your table in the freshest possible condition.

Second, slow food members view eating as a social event. They believe we should take pleasure in gathering and preparing our food. We should share our food with friends and family and eating should be enjoyed as a social occasion. These days everyone is in a hurry and more and more families are sacrificing meal times together in order to fit more activities into an already hectic schedule. Food is something to be savored and enjoyed according to the slow food movement. It can bring people together.

Third, the slow food movement is dedicated to educating children about where their food comes from and how it is grown, as well as giving them more tastes to experience. The slow food movement is not necessarily the same thing as eating organically, but some of their principles overlap. And because slow food proponents tend to support farmers who are gentle to the earth, they often use food grown organically. Educating children about how food is grown, as well as the drawbacks of pesticides, preservatives, and certain big-farming practices, will eventually lead to healthy adults who appreciate the many tastes and textures of their region.

The slow food movement is not without its opponents, of course. One of the major problems cited by those opposed to the slow food movement is cost. Because slow food is focused on eating local, often organic, cuisine, many feel that the lifestyle is unrealistic and expensive. Most families can't afford to eat organically all the time, and, as a result, the movement has been labeled as being for the "elite." The slow food movement has responded to this criticism by taking a bigger interest in politics and asking for a complete reform of the agricultural industry. Members of the movement insist that the cost issue points to a need for an overhaul of the system. Something is wrong, they insist, if only the "elite" can afford to eat healthy food. It's hard to argue with that.

1.   **What are the main goals of the slow food movement?**

_____

_____

_____

_____

_____

2.   What is one problem with the slow food movement?

   _____

   _____

   _____

   _____

   _____

3.   Should more people embrace the slow food movement? Why or why not?

   _____

   _____

   _____

   _____

   _____

   _____

Discussion

Your teacher will split you into small groups. Discuss your responses to Numbers 1 through 3. Take turns sharing your responses and listening to the responses of others. At least one student should take notes on your discussion.

When you are finished with your discussion, answer the questions on the next page as a group. Choose one group member to present your group's responses to the class.

✔ **A good discussion participant:**

☐ builds on others' ideas.

☐ expresses ideas clearly.

☐ comes to discussions prepared.

☐ refers to evidence on the topic, text, or issue.

☐ tracks progress toward specific goals and deadlines.

☐ fulfills individual roles as needed.

☐ poses questions.

☐ responds to others' questions and comments.

☐ keeps discussion on topic.

☐ recognizes new information.

☐ modifies personal views, when necessary.

Summary

1. Did everyone in your group share the same opinion about slow food? Explain.

    _____

    _____

    _____

    _____

    _____

2. What were the <u>best</u> reasons given for each side of the argument?

    _____

    _____

    _____

    _____

    _____

    _____

Lesson 22: Speaking

Speaking in front of a group can be intimidating, no doubt. But there are a few things you can do to be well prepared, which will help ease any anxiety you might have. Follow the tips in this lesson, and you'll be speaking in front of crowds and persuading people in no time.

 ## TIP 1: Speak clearly and confidently.

Think about the best speaker you've ever heard. Did he or she look down at the podium the whole time, never making eye contact? What about volume? Did you have to strain to hear his or her voice? Were the words clear or was there definite mumbling going on? How you speak is just as important as what you say. Even the best speeches can be derailed by a speaker who mumbles through the material.

Here are a few suggestions that will help.

- **Speak up.** Make sure your volume is appropriate for the size of the room you'll be speaking in. If you're speaking in front of your class, think about your teacher's voice during lectures. Make sure everyone in the room can hear you, including those in the back row. This doesn't mean you should yell—just project.

- **Practice your pronunciation.** Does this ever happen to you? You try to say something and find yourself tripping over the words, and by the time you spit it out, you know you've lost your audience? Don't let it happen when you're giving a speech.

  One of the best ways to avoid this is to practice, practice, practice. When you practice your speech, you learn the rhythm and cadence of your material. You become comfortable with it. You'll be able to identify problem areas, and either change your wording or master the problem.

  Speaking clearly will enable your audience to better understand you. You can't influence an audience if they don't know what you're saying. And clear pronunciation will make you seem more confident, which leads us to our next piece of advice.

- **Be confident.** There are clubs and societies that exist solely to help people master their fear of public speaking. It's one of the most common fears out there, actually. So if you're intimidated at the thought of standing in front of a group and expressing yourself, don't worry: you're not alone. If you follow the two suggestions above, you'll already feel more confident. Speaking up and speaking clearly will go a long ways toward convincing your audience that you are confident and that you believe in what you're saying. If you are not confident about your argument, how can your audience be?

- **Make eye contact.** No one wants to sit through a 10-minute speech where the speaker mumbles into note cards the whole time. Speaking is about connecting with your audience. The quickest and easiest way to do this is by making eye contact. Know what you want to say, but don't rely on note cards for your entire speech. This will free your eyes from looking at your notes the whole time. Make sure you look at your audience and engage with them. They will trust you and be more likely to agree with what you are saying.

 TIP 2: Use visual aids when appropriate.

Computers, slides, maps, graphs. All of these things can enhance your presentation and make it more interesting. Don't be shy about using visual aids when speaking. Most listeners appreciate being given something to look at. Visual aids can be used to help make an issue more clear, or to illustrate a particular point. For example, imagine you're giving a speech about Lewis and Clark. You could use a map to show the route they took to reach the Pacific Ocean. You could show pictures of the travelers and their guides. You could even bring in an example of the type of compass they might have used. Visual aids can back up your facts and will help grab your audience's interest.

Computers are a great source for visual aids, too. You can find pictures online or even create PowerPoint presentations to enhance your speech.

1. You have been asked to give a speech on global warming. What visual aids could you use with your speech?

_____

_____

_____

_____

2. What visual aids could you use for a speech about French traditions in Canada?

_____

_____

_____

_____

TIP 3: Adapt your speech to your audience.

Remember Lesson 8, when you learned how important it is to know your audience when writing? It is just as important when speaking. You should use formal English when speaking in a formal setting, like in school. You can be more casual if you are speaking to a group of your peers.

3. You are giving a speech to the school board to persuade them not to cut funding for your favorite after-school activity. What should the tone of your speech be? What language should you use?

_____

_____

_____

_____

4. You are giving a speech to your classmates in support of your friend Tom's campaign for class president. What should the tone of your speech be? What language would you use?

_____

_____

_____

_____

Lesson Practice begins on the following page.

Directions: This passage is about the troubles facing public libraries in the United States. Read the passage. Then respond to the prompt.

The Right to Read

by Sara Sullivan

There is some debate about which was the first public library in the United States. The Darby Free Library, in Darby, Pennsylvania, which has been open since 1743, claims to be the longest continuously operating library in the nation. The Boston Public Library claims to be the first major tax-supported free library in the United States. (It was also the first library in the United States to have a designated space for children.) The Franklin Public Library claims to be America's first lending library.

These little distinctions could go on forever, and ultimately they're not that important, but it is easy to see why different libraries would want to claim the title. Libraries date back thousands of years, from ancient Mesopotamia to the Great Library of Alexandria, to Caesar's Rome. Libraries have long been a symbol of intellectual curiosity and pursuit. What could be nobler?

Despite such a rich history, today's libraries aren't exactly experiencing a golden age. There are several factors contributing to the trouble faced by public libraries, meaning there will not be one easy fix. The main problem is that public libraries rely on various government funds to operate. In the past few decades, funding has been slashed as cities and states deal with serious budget issues. This has resulted in hours and services being cut, and library branches being closed altogether.

Libraries are also facing rising operating costs in the face of budget cuts. For one thing, the cost of books and magazines has risen. Not only are printed materials more expensive, but libraries are also charged with maintaining computer equipment and networks. It actually takes quite a bit of money to provide all of the free services and amenities found at public libraries.

There are those who view libraries as antiquated institutions not meant to function in a modern age. With the advent of the Internet, libraries are no longer the only option for in-depth research. But this kind of narrow view disregards a very important fact: not everyone can afford Internet access at home. And libraries offer more than just books. People who are out of work use the public computers to conduct job searches, or visit the library for resume writing tips or practice interviews. In this capacity, the library serves a vital public function. And there are many people whose only access to books comes from a library. A free library card can open up entire worlds through literature that many people might not otherwise be exposed to. Most public libraries also loan music and movies, creating a low-cost alternative for family entertainment. Branch libraries in cities are available for people who do not have their own transportation.

Libraries all across the nation are in danger. Townspeople have banded together and tried everything to keep them open, from collecting donations to forming "Save Our Library" committees to appealing to congressmen. It is clear that without drastic action, these institutions, upon which so many people depend, will be lost.

Speaking

Plan a speech in which you explain what should be done to help save public libraries.

Directions: Write notes for your speech in the space below.

Using your notes on the previous page, you will present your speech to your class. Your teacher will give you specific instructions for your presentation.

Speaker's Checklist

✔ **A good presenter:**

☐ emphasizes important points with descriptions and details.

☐ makes eye contact with the audience.

☐ speaks at a reasonable volume.

☐ clearly pronounces words, using formal English.

☐ uses digital media and visual displays of data, when possible.

Mechanics Toolbox

Pronouns

A **pronoun** is a word that takes the place of a noun. The form of a pronoun shows both person and number.

Person refers to the point of view expressed by the pronoun: first person (the person speaking, or *I*), second person (the person spoken to, or *you*), or third person (the person or thing spoken of, or *he, she,* or *it*).

Number refers to how many people or things the pronoun represents. A **singular** pronoun represents one person or thing. A **plural** pronoun represents more than one person or thing.

This chart features the personal pronouns.

	Singular	Plural
First Person	I, me	we, us
Second Person	you	you
Third Person	he, him; she, her; it	they, them

An **antecedent** is the word that a pronoun replaces. Pronouns and antecedents need to agree in person and number. Third-person singular pronouns and antecedents also need to agree in gender. The antecedent for a pronoun may appear in a previous sentence. It may also appear earlier within the same sentence as the pronoun.

> Examples:
> My class organized a fundraiser. We raised nearly $10,000! (correct)
> After Susan and Elfranko finished the laundry, they went swimming. (correct)
> When a person does well on this exam, they should be congratulated. (incorrect)

In the fourth example, the plural pronoun, *they*, does not agree with the singular antecedent, *person*. The correct sentence is:

> When people do well on this exam, they should be congratulated.

It also needs to be clear which noun is the antecedent of a pronoun. Consider this example:

> We piled tall stacks of books on the tables until they fell over.

The antecedent of *they* is not clear. Did the stacks of books fall over, or did the tables? It is best not to use a pronoun in this sentence. The correct possibilities are:

> We piled tall stacks of books on the tables until the books fell over.
> We piled tall stacks of books on the tables until the tables fell over.

Mechanics Toolbox

258

Sentence Pattern

A sentence is a group of words that tells a complete thought. It can stand alone. It can include various combinations of clauses and phrases, but it has at least one subject and predicate. The **subject** tells who or what the sentence is about. The **predicate** tells what the subject does.

> Example:
> They left.

They is the subject of this sentence. The predicate is *left.* It tells what they did.

 Phrases and Clauses

A **phrase** is a group of related words that does not include its own subject and verb. A comma should follow an introductory phrase. For example:

> Examples:
> From the very first day, Tabitha liked her new school. (prepositional phrase)
> Walking on tiptoe, James creeped behind his little sister. (participial phrase)
> To tell you the truth, I did not like that movie at all. (infinitive phrase)
> A sleepy town next to nowhere, Riverdale was beautiful. (appositive phrase)

A **clause** is a group of words that includes a subject and verb. There are two types of clauses: independent clauses and dependent clauses.

An **independent clause** can stand alone as a sentence. It tells a complete thought. In the following examples, each subject is underlined once, and each verb is underlined twice.

> We argued.
> George agreed to walk his neighbor's retriever.
> They practiced hard that entire year.

Although it includes both a subject and verb, a **dependent clause** cannot stand alone. It is not complete. Some dependent clauses begin with a relative pronoun, such as *who, whom, which,* or *that.* The relative pronoun may serve as the subject of the dependent clause. Other dependent clauses begin with a subordinating conjunction, such as *after, although, because, however, if, until,* and *when.* In the following examples, each subject is underlined once, and each verb is underlined twice.

> Until we started to laugh.
> Although he dislikes dogs.
> Which ended with their first championship.

Mechanics Toolbox

On its own, none of these clauses expresses a complete thought. It needs to be joined to an independent clause.

Examples:
We argued until we started to laugh.
Although he dislikes dogs, George agreed to walk his neighbor's retriever.
They practiced hard that entire year, which ended with their first championship.

 ## Compound Subjects and Predicates

A sentence can include more than one subject. For example:

Yolanda enjoys reading. Ursula enjoys reading, too.

These sentences can be combined into one sentence with a compound subject.

Example:
Yolanda and Ursula enjoy reading.

Notice the change in the verb when the sentences are combined. The compound subject, *Yolanda and Ursula*, needs a plural verb, *enjoy*.

A sentence can also include more than one predicate. For example:

Yolanda enjoyed that book. She did not like the movie based on it.

These sentences can be combined into one sentence with a compound verb.

Example:
Yolanda enjoyed that book but did not like the movie based on it.

Yolanda is the subject of both predicates, *enjoyed that book* and *did not like the movie based on it.*

A sentence can have both a compound subject and a compound verb. For example:

Yolanda and Ursula enjoyed that book and are looking forward to reading the sequel.

Both subjects, *Yolanda* and *Ursula*, are the subject of both predicates, *enjoyed that book* and *are looking forward to reading the sequel.*

Mechanics Toolbox

Types of Sentences

Different combinations of independent and dependent clauses form different types of sentences. There are four basic sentence patterns.

1. A **simple sentence** includes one independent clause and no dependent clauses.

   Examples:
   The lilies bloomed.
   The violinist amazed the audience with her skill.
   When did you return home?

2. A **compound sentence** includes two or more independent clauses. In the following examples, each independent clause is underlined.

   Michael lost his wallet, but a stranger soon returned it to him.
   We could get the books at the library, or my sister will lend us her copies.
   I wrote the lead article, Amy did the interviews, and Jimmy designed the layout.

3. A **complex sentence** includes one independent clause and one or more dependent clauses. In the following examples, each independent clause is underlined once, and each dependent clause is underlined twice.

   Our basement floods whenever it rains.
   The dress that my mother made is my favorite.
   Because Lisa usually visits him on Saturday, her grandfather worried when he did not see her that weekend.

Notice that the dependent clause *that my mother made* appears between the subject and verb of the independent clause *The dress is my favorite.*

4. A **compound-complex sentence** includes two or more independent clauses and at least one dependent clause. In the following examples, each independent clause is underlined once, and each dependent clause is underlined twice.

   Although they had never taken care of a garden before, their flowers were healthy and their vegetables were delicious.
   Whenever Allison practices the clarinet, her dog starts barking and the stray cats that live in the empty lot behind her house start yowling.

Notice that the dependent clause *that live in the empty lot behind her house* appears between the subject and verb of the independent clause *the stray cats start yowling.*

Mechanics Toolbox

Concise Words and Phrases

Good writers choose their words carefully. They use vivid words that appeal to the senses. They also use words that convey precise meanings. Consider these examples:

I was hot. (general word choice)
Sweat poured into my eyes. (vivid word choice)

The second sentence is more vivid. It helps the reader feel the speaker's discomfort in the heat. Using the verb *poured,* it is more active. It is best to avoid overusing forms of the verb *be,* such as *was* in the first sentence.

Consider these other examples:

Swimming in the <u>water</u> <u>made me feel better</u>. (vague word choice)
Swimming in the <u>lake</u> <u>cooled me off</u>. (precise word choice)

In fewer words, the second sentence conveys much more detail than the first. It tells precisely where the speaker went swimming: in a lake. It also tells precisely how the speaker felt better: he or she cooled off.

It is usually better to use a vivid verb or precise noun than add an adjective or adverb. Here are examples:

Holly <u>walked quickly</u> across the parking lot. (verb and adverb)
Holly <u>hurried</u> across the parking lot. (vivid verb)

Also avoid adjectives or adverbs that repeat ideas already conveyed through other words. For example:

Neil Gaiman, my favorite writer, has written a wide variety of different books.

It is not necessary to use both *variety* and *different* in this sentence. The word *variety* on its own conveys the idea of difference. This sentence is better:

Neil Gaiman, my favorite writer, has written a wide variety of books.

Mechanics Toolbox

Verb Voice and Mood

In a sentence that reflects the **active voice**, the actor is the subject. In a sentence that reflects the **passive voice**, the object of an action is the subject. Compare these examples:

> My aunt donated the costumes for the performance. (active voice)
> The costumes for the performance were donated by my aunt. (passive voice)

My aunt is the subject of the first sentence. She is doing the donating. *The costumes* is the subject of the second sentence. They are the object of the donating.

The active voice is generally preferred. However, there may be times when the passive voice is acceptable or even necessary. For example, you might use the passive voice in a letter of complaint if you do not want to write a direct accusation:

> We have learned that some children were prevented from seeing the performance.

You might need to use the passive voice if the actor is unknown. For example:

> The flowers for the performance were also donated. We have no idea who sent them.

Conditional sentences tell about events that are dependent on a condition that may or may not occur. The condition is given in a dependent clause beginning with *if*. The possible consequence of the condition is given in the independent clause.

The tense and mood of the verbs in a conditional sentence depend on the truth of the condition given in the sentence. The condition may be true, possibly true, or untrue.

> If we <u>have</u> ice cream, we <u>are</u> happy. (true about the present)
> If we <u>have</u> ice cream, we <u>will be</u> happy. (true about the future)
> If we <u>have</u> ice cream, we <u>should be</u> happy. (possibly true about the future)
> If we <u>had</u> ice cream, we <u>would be</u> happy. (untrue about the present)

Notice the verbs in the independent clauses of the sentences about possibly true or untrue conditions. They are in the **conditional mood** and include the helping verbs *should* and *would*. The conditional mood expresses possible but uncertain events. The helping verbs *could* or *might* can also be used in the conditional mood.

Also notice the past-tense verb (*had*) in the dependent clause that expresses an untrue condition. This verb is in the **subjunctive mood**. The subjunctive mood expresses untrue or hypothetical events. It is often used in clauses beginning with *if* or to express wishes. For example:

> If I <u>were</u> you, I would give up now.
> I wish I <u>were</u> in charge.

Mechanics Toolbox

Notes